RESURRECTION ACADEMY

Across Five Aprils

and Related Readings

McDougal Littell
A HOUGHTON MIFFLIN COMPANY

Evanston, Illinois   *Boston   Dallas*

Acknowledgments

Houghton Mifflin Company: "Prison Bars and the Surgeon's Saw," from *The Boys' War* by Jim Murphy; Copyright © 1990 by Jim Murphy. Reprinted by permission of Clarion Books/Houghton Mifflin Company. All rights reserved.

"The Mysterious Mr. Lincoln," from *Lincoln: A Photobiography* by Russell Freedman; Copyright © 1987 by Russell Freedman. Reprinted by permission of Clarion Books/Houghton Mifflin Company. All rights reserved.

"Around the Campfire," from *After the Lost War* by Andrew Hudgins; Copyright © 1988 by Andrew Hudgins. Reprinted by permission of Houghton Mifflin Company. All rights reserved.

Don Congdon Associates, Inc.: "The Drummer Boy of Shiloh," by Ray Bradbury, originally published in the *Saturday Evening Post* in 1960; Copyright © 1960 by Ray Bradbury; Copyright renewed © 1988. Reprinted by permission of Don Congdon Associates, Inc.

W. W. Norton & Company, Inc.: "The Huts at Esquimax," from *The Springhouse* by Norman Dubie; Copyright © 1986 by Norman Dubie. Reprinted by permission of W. W. Norton & Company, Inc.

Random House UK Ltd.: "The Sniper," from *The Short Stories of Liam O'Flaherty*. Reprinted by permission of the Estate of Liam O'Flaherty and of Jonathon Cape Ltd., a division of Random House UK Ltd.

HarperCollins Publishers, Inc.: Excerpts from *Voices from the Civil War* by Milton Meltzer; Copyright © 1989 by Milton Meltzer. Reprinted by permission of HarperCollins Publishers, Inc.

Across Five Aprils by Irene Hunt, Copyright © 1964 by Irene Hunt. Published by Modern Curriculum Press, an imprint of Simon & Schuster, Elementary Division. Reprinted by arrangement with Modern Curriculum Press. All rights reserved.

Illustration by Michael Steirnagle.

Contents

Across Five Aprils

Irene Hunt

Chapter 1

ELLEN Creighton and her nine-year-old son, Jethro, were planting potatoes in the half-acre just south of their cabin that morning in mid-April, 1861; they were out in the field as soon as breakfast was over, and southern Illinois at that hour was pink with sunrise and swelling redbud and clusters of bloom over the apple orchard across the road. Jethro walked on the warm clods of plowed earth and felt them crumble beneath his feet as he helped his mother carry the tub of potato cuttings they had prepared the night before.

"It's damp fur down and warm on top," he remarked, poking a brown hand deep into the soil. "Once we git these planted and a soft rain comes, we'll hev a crop to make people up north call us 'Egypt' fer sure."

He filled a burlap pouch with the potato cuttings and hoisted it expertly to his thin shoulder where a batch of new freckles was just beginning to appear. The world seemed a good place to him that morning, and he felt ready to stride down the length of the field with a firm step and a joke on his lips.

"Do you reckon we'll be through by the time ham and corn bread is ready fer dinner, Mis' Creighton?" he asked grinning. He called her "Mis' Creighton" sometimes as his older brothers did when they teased her; it was just a step from the too-bold joke of addressing her by her given name.

His mother smiled back at him, acknowledging his mood, but she shook her head at his words.

"Yore hopes is makin' a fool of yore reason, Jeth.

We're lucky if these 'taters is bedded tomorrow."

She made short, quick cuts with her h
mellow soil and waited until Jethro placed
eye upward, in the spot hollowed out for
which she raked a covering of soil over it an
down the long furrow.

She was a small, spare woman with large
and skin as brown and dry as leather. She ha
pretty girl back in the 1830's when she
Matthew Creighton, but prettiness was sh
among country women of her time; she did
much about it anymore except now and th
Jenny's fourteen-year-old radiance was e
compelling. Even if she had been concerne
were reverberations of Calvinism strong wit
which would have protested vigorously aga
vanity of regret for a passing beauty. She ha
twelve children, four of whom were dead
five, for the oldest son had not been heard fro
he left for the goldfields of California twel
before; she had lived through sickness, pove
danger for over thirty years; the sight of a pre
might bring a tired smile to her lips, but it
thing of little value in Ellen's world.

Jethro was her youngest child, born in the
'52, a year in which three of her children died
one week of the dreaded disease they called
paralysis, a disease which struck the count
year, people said, like the soldiers of Herod
knew that she favored her youngest son, th
overlooked shortcomings in Jethro for whi
older children had been punished. It was a we
of her advancing years, she supposed, but th
the son who had been spared that summer
children all around were dying of the ag

Across Five Aprils

Irene Hunt

Chapter 1

ELLEN Creighton and her nine-year-old son, Jethro, were planting potatoes in the half-acre just south of their cabin that morning in mid-April, 1861; they were out in the field as soon as breakfast was over, and southern Illinois at that hour was pink with sunrise and swelling redbud and clusters of bloom over the apple orchard across the road. Jethro walked on the warm clods of plowed earth and felt them crumble beneath his feet as he helped his mother carry the tub of potato cuttings they had prepared the night before.

"It's damp fur down and warm on top," he remarked, poking a brown hand deep into the soil. "Once we git these planted and a soft rain comes, we'll hev a crop to make people up north call us 'Egypt' fer sure."

He filled a burlap pouch with the potato cuttings and hoisted it expertly to his thin shoulder where a batch of new freckles was just beginning to appear. The world seemed a good place to him that morning, and he felt ready to stride down the length of the field with a firm step and a joke on his lips.

"Do you reckon we'll be through by the time ham and corn bread is ready fer dinner, Mis' Creighton?" he asked grinning. He called her "Mis' Creighton" sometimes as his older brothers did when they teased her; it was just a step from the too-bold joke of addressing her by her given name.

His mother smiled back at him, acknowledging his mood, but she shook her head at his words.

"Yore hopes is makin' a fool of yore reason, Jeth.

We're lucky if these 'taters is bedded by noon tomorrow."

She made short, quick cuts with her hoe in the mellow soil and waited until Jethro placed a cutting, eye upward, in the spot hollowed out for it, after which she raked a covering of soil over it and moved down the long furrow.

She was a small, spare woman with large dark eyes and skin as brown and dry as leather. She had been a pretty girl back in the 1830's when she married Matthew Creighton, but prettiness was short-lived among country women of her time; she didn't think much about it anymore except now and then when Jenny's fourteen-year-old radiance was especially compelling. Even if she had been concerned, there were reverberations of Calvinism strong within her, which would have protested vigorously against the vanity of regret for a passing beauty. She had borne twelve children, four of whom were dead—perhaps five, for the oldest son had not been heard from since he left for the goldfields of California twelve years before; she had lived through sickness, poverty, and danger for over thirty years; the sight of a pretty face might bring a tired smile to her lips, but it was a thing of little value in Ellen's world.

Jethro was her youngest child, born in the year of '52, a year in which three of her children died within one week of the dreaded disease they called child's paralysis, a disease which struck the country that year, people said, like the soldiers of Herod. Ellen knew that she favored her youngest son, that she overlooked shortcomings in Jethro for which her older children had been punished. It was a weakness of her advancing years, she supposed, but this was the son who had been spared that summer when children all around were dying of the agonizing sickness; it looked as if, somehow, Destiny had marked him. One didn't talk about such things; the world, she knew, was impatient with women who value their own children too highly. Ellen kept her silence, but she saw signs of special talents in Jethro, and she watched over him with special tenderness.

They worked together for an hour or more without speaking. Ellen was grave and absorbed in the anxious thoughts of that spring; Jethro was accustomed to adapting himself to the behaviors and moods of older people, and he found enough in the world about him to occupy his interest as he worked. A south breeze brought the scent of lilacs and sweet fennel to his nostrils and set all the frosty-green leaves of a silver poplar tree to trembling. There was a column of wood-smoke feathering up from the kitchen chimney, a sign that Jenny was already making preparations for a hearty noon meal. From the neighboring field across the creek he could hear the shouted commands to the plow horses as Matt Creighton and his two older sons got on with the spring plowing. It was a fine morning; many people around him were troubled, he knew, but that was a part of the adult world which he accepted as a matter of course. Adults were usually troubled. There were chinch bugs and grasshoppers, months of drought, elections, slavery, secession, talk of war—the adult world of trouble, though, was not real enough to dim the goodness of an April morning.

At about seven o'clock a team and wagon pulled out of the barnlot, stopping for a minute before turning into the road while the driver spoke to a girl who came running out of the kitchen door.

Jethro chuckled. "Shad's leavin' fer Newton now, I guess. Jenny has to say good-bye like as if he was goin' to the North Pole."

He watched the wagon from the corner of his eye as he worked, and when the team started coming down the road toward the potato patch, he put the heavy bag of cuttings aside and raced across the field to the roadside. His mother laid down her hoe and followed slowly, picking her way over the mounds of plowed earth that Jethro's feet seemed barely to touch.

The young schoolmaster stopped the team and climbed down from the wagon to stand at the fencerow waiting for Jethro and Ellen to come up from midfield. He was a tall, powerfully built youth of twenty, with a firm mouth and grave, dark eyes that gave him the appearance of an older man. He had come out from Pennsylvania three years earlier to study at McKendree College, where an uncle was professor of natural philosophy, a subject that later generations would call physics. Faced with insufficient funds to carry on his studies at the end of his first year, young Yale had turned to the country schools as a stepping-stone toward further work in college, and a series of circumstances had led him to the school for which Matt Creighton served as a director. Here he had stayed, not just one year as originally planned, but two, and now in 1861 he had hired himself out as a farmhand to Matt for the summer and contracted to teach still a third term that fall.

He had been stricken with typhoid fever during his first year of teaching, and Ellen Creighton had patiently nursed him back to health with the skill she had learned over the years. There was a strong tie of affection between the two of them; Ellen counted Shadrach as a part of her family and looked after him as she did her own, and Shadrach Yale, in turn, showed a thoughtful courtesy for her that few women of the prairies received from their own sons.

"Will you be back by suppertime, Shad?" Jethro called breathlessly as he approached the fencerow.

At school he addressed the young teacher as "Master," but now that Shadrach was so much a member of the family the necessary formalities of a schoolroom were forgotten.

"It's not likely, Jeth, not before nine or maybe later."

Shadrach smiled at the thin eager face turned up to him. He was mature enough at twenty to appreciate being a hero to a nine-year-old boy; besides that, Jethro's quick mind and delight in learning had been a source of pleasure for studious young Yale, who had known the frustration of trying to penetrate the apathy and unconcern of a backwoods classroom. He had talked to both parents about the promise he recognized in the boy; Matt, in spite of his pleasure, had shaken his head and wondered if the praise for Jethro had not stemmed from interest in Jethro's sister, Jenny. But Ellen had felt no doubts; the praise was in line with what she herself believed firmly.

She stood beside the gray rails that morning with her hands folded beneath her apron. Matt had made a pretext of needing supplies from town, but she knew that this trip to Newton in the midst of a late planting season would have been unthinkable except for the urgency of getting word from the world beyond their own fields and woods pastures. Her face looked drawn in the bright sunlight.

"I wisht there was a telegraph in Newton, Shad," she said.

He nodded. "There's one in Olney; they'll send any important news on up to Newton as soon as it comes through. At any rate I'll bring the latest papers."

"Seems sometimes there's a deep silence all about us out here waitin' to be filled." She and the young man looked at one another, each pair of eyes dark with anxiety.

Jethro kicked a stone in the road. "Sure wisht I was goin' to town with you, Shad," he said finally, because it seemed that someone *must* say something.

"I know. Well, there'll be other trips this summer, Jeth."

Shadrach started to climb back into the wagon as he spoke; then, changing his mind, he turned back and placed his hands quickly on Ellen's shoulders. "Try not to worry," he said quietly.

The caress brought sudden tears to her eyes. She and Jethro stood watching as he drove away; when the wagon disappeared in a clump of trees at a bend in the road, Ellen turned back to her work slowly as if overwhelmed by a deep weariness.

"The Lord knows what news he'll bring back," she said. "There may be war in the land at this minute fer all we know."

Jethro was depressed by her somber mood, but not by the imminence of war. He had listened to his brother Tom and their cousin Eb, the two younger of the grown boys in the household, and their excitement had found its way into his blood. Dread of war was a womanly weakness, he had discovered, evidenced by his mother's melancholy and the tears of Jenny and his brother John's wife, Nancy.

"I heered some of the big fellers talkin' the other night, and they said the war, even if it comes, will be no more than a breakfas' spell. They said that soldiers up here kin take the South by the britches and make it holler 'Nough' quicker than it takes coffee to cool off fer swallerin'."

Jethro spoke hurriedly, almost sure that the words

would anger his mother and vaguely realizing that he wanted to anger her a little for spoiling the brightness of the morning by her obvious sadness.

She had a way of closing her eyes briefly when exasperated as if to reject for at least a second the existence of a folly that she was bound to recognize later. Her hoe jabbed deeper and more sharply into the brown earth at her feet.

"They're foolish young 'uns, and they're talkin' without a spark of reason to guide their words," she said angrily. "It ain't that I don't love 'em—big talk or not," she added, "but I'm fearful of the day when they face their comeuppance. I'm fearful of the time when I'll hev no boys left but you—and the three little ones up on Walnut Hill."

Jethro squirmed inwardly. If there were going to be tears and talk of the children who had died the summer he was born, he wanted to escape. And since one didn't easily escape from his mother in the midst of planting a half-acre of potatoes, he searched hurriedly for a way to turn the conversation.

"Did ever I tell you, Ma, of an old feller that give all the people of the earth their comeuppance?" he asked brightly, knowing that she was always proud to hear of the things he'd learned from Shadrach at school.

"I reckon you didn't, Jeth, not that I'm able to recollect."

Jethro straightened his shoulders a little under the weight upon them.

"Well, ma'am, there was a long time when people allowed that the earth was the big kingpin amongst all the stars and things. They thought that the moon and sun and all the stars went 'round the earth and maybe kind of tipped their hats as they went by. Shad says that most everybody went on believin' that fer years till finally there come along this man I'm tellin' you about. He was head and shoulders smarter than the run of the mill, and after he'd watched the sun and moon and stars fer a long time he set down and he done some figgerin'. Well, when he got through figgerin' he showed it to some other fellers and there it was, plain as anything—the earth *wasn't* the big kingpin at all. He allowed it was jest a little old star chasin' 'round the sun with a pack of others, some of 'em a lot bigger than us. Shad says that some folks took that news real hard; it kind of let the wind out of their sails all of a sudden."

"That ain't in the Scriptures, is it, Jeth?"

"I don't reckon so, but it's in one of the books Shad brought out from Philadelphy."

His mother looked thoughtful. "The Lord God created the earth and all upon it, Jeth. I don't like to hear that His work warn't of the best."

"But don't you see, Ma, He created the sun and moon and stars too—some a little bigger, others maybe a little purtier. Seems like people on earth believed *we* had the best diggin's jest because we wanted to believe that—because it made us feel important—"

"You ain't watchin' to keep the 'tater eyes facin' up, Jeth," Ellen said quietly, pointing with the tip of her hoe.

He stooped and turned a cutting over. "Guess I kind of got carried away with my own noise," he said flushing.

Her eyes lighted a little. "Well, you done me a favor—tellin' me things I ain't never learned and givin' me somethin' to ponder over. It 'mazes me, Jeth, it does fer a fact, the way you kin recollect all the things Shad tells you and how you kin put them from his way of talkin' into mine."

She hoed in silence for a minute and then paid him the great compliment of going back to his story.

"Did you tell me what the old feller's name was, the one that done all the figgerin'?"

"His name was Copernicus. I kin even spell it fer you if you're a mind. Shad made me learn how to say it and spell it too."

"Sounds like a furriner."

Jethro nodded. "I allow," he agreed.

Ellen sighed. "Seems like furriners is allus stirrin' up somethin'. Well, the pot can't call the kettle black—look what we're stirrin' up amongst ourselves."

She was back to the problems of the times, and Jethro knew that he could not tempt her away from them. For months he had moved along the edge of the furor that raged among the adults of his family, of the neighborhood, and even of the church. He knew that there had been fights in the neighborhood, anger and triumph over the election of President Lincoln in the fall of '60, but he supposed, if he thought of it at all, that this was the natural behavior of people interested in a vague thing called politics. He had heard talk of tariffs, of slave states and free ones, of a violent old man named John Brown, and during the past winter, of states seceding from the Union. But it had just been talk to him, and the only part of all the talk that held any interest for him was the conviction among all the men that war was sure to break out sooner or later. It hadn't broken out yet, however, and some men were swearing because the President had not declared war, while others were saying, "Jest let Ol' Abe fire on the South and watch Kentucky, Missouri, Tennessee—yes, and maybe southern Illinois—tumble over on the Confederate side of the fence."

He knew a little about wars. The Revolution, of course. The *American* Revolution, Shadrach had pointed out, and Jethro had been amazed that there was ever any other. He liked stories of wars. There was a beautiful one described in one of Shad's books in which an ancient king watched ships fight in a place called Salamis Bay; there was another exciting story of a battle in which small, fast ships with the lucky help of a violent storm had played Old Ned with a proud and mighty navy. He wanted to tell his mother about that one, how if the battle had gone the other way, both Ellen and Jethro Creighton might well have been speaking Spanish as they planted their potatoes that April morning.

She wouldn't have liked that though; she was suspicious of people who spoke a different language. Well, one learned when to speak and when to keep one's tongue between his teeth. Jethro was not going to talk to his mother too much of either languages or wars, but he knew that, as far as the latter were concerned, he was one with young Tom and Eb when they hoped that war would come soon. War meant loud brass music and shining horses ridden by men wearing uniforms finer than any suit in the stores at Newton; it meant men riding like kings, looking neither to the right nor the left, while lesser men in perfect lines strode along with guns across their shoulders, their heads held high like horses with short reins. When the battle thundered and exploded on all sides—well, some men were killed, of course, but the stories of war that Jethro remembered were about the men who had managed to live through the thunder and explosion. Matt Creighton's grandfather had lived through the Revolution; Matt himself had survived the Mexican War; and Uncle Billy Jeffers, down the road, was still alive to tell tales of the War of 1812. Jethro, forgetting the lecture to his mother on the inclination of people to select beliefs that bring them most satisfaction, never doubted that if Tom and Eb got their chance to go to war, they'd be back home when it was over, and that it would be shadowy men from distant parts who would die for the pages of future history books.

Death, however, was neither simple nor lightly brushed aside when it struck home. Jethro frowned; he didn't like to think of his sister Mary's death, but some memory had been touched off as his thoughts wandered. Let a few hours of work go by and let one's body begin to weary a little—then the thoughts that had been all of beauty and spring a while before started turning to things that were better forgotten. He had not forgotten though; he'd been only seven that winter of '59, but the memory of the tragedy would always be sharp and terrible in his mind.

Mary had been as pretty as Jenny, only blond and more delicate. Jethro remembered that it was a bitter night and that he had stood with his nose pressed against the cold windowpane watching Rob Nelson help her into the wagon before they left for a dance over toward Hidalgo. What happened later he'd pieced together from loud outcries and scraps of conversation deep in the middle of the night.

It seemed that a crowd of young toughs from the south of the county had broken uninvited into the dance, waving whiskey bottles and shouting drunken insults at the guests. As things began to look more and more dangerous, Rob found Mary's wraps, and they were starting for home when a drunken youth named Travis Burdow saw them leave and followed them on horseback.

Rob told Matt Creighton how he had urged the team, hoping to get to Ed Turner's farm where he could get help, because he knew that Burdow was armed. Rob had succeeded in getting as far as Turner's driveway when Burdow, seeing that his game was about finished, rode up beside Rob's team and fired a pistol over the heads of the horses. The frightened animals bolted through a rail fence, overturning the wagon and kicking themselves loose from the tongue. Mary was dead when Rob and Ed Turner pulled her from the wreckage.

The countryside was in an uproar the next day when news of the tragedy got around. Matthew Creighton was held in high esteem by his neighbors, and the senseless killing of his daughter stirred up a rage that was heightened by the fact that the whole Burdow family was commonly despised throughout the countryside as a shiftless lot with a bad background.

The grandfather of Travis Burdow had come from somewhere farther downstate, and when he moved into Jasper County he came hurriedly, in order, so the story went, to escape a mob of citizens whose anger during years of petty thieving had exploded over the theft of a team of horses from a prosperous farmer. Whether the story was true or not, suspicion and dislike settled upon the family, and thirty years had failed to dissipate it. The Burdow children were nicknamed "Jail Burd-ows" by taunting schoolmates and persecuted in a hundred petty ways. Dave Burdow, father of young Travis and son of the alleged horse thief, was a sullen, silent man who shunned people in general and accepted their insults as a matter of course when he was forced to deal with them. His sons, for the most part, were much like him except when liquor quickened their courage and defiance. The shot that Travis Burdow fired over Rob Nelson's team that night was a shot fired at a society that had kicked a boy from childhood on because he bore his grandfather's name.

And so the anger of the mob at Mary's death was doubled and tripled because a Burdow was responsible. By late afternoon, a crowd of fifty or more armed men stopped at the Creighton cabin to tell Matt of their intention of hunting Travis Burdow down and hanging him on the spot. But Matt Creighton had intervened, and it was a mark of the respect he commanded in the community that the men listened as he stood for an hour in the icy afternoon pleading with them to keep their hands free of further bloodshed.

Jethro, understanding the situation more fully now that he was older, wondered at his father's intervention that afternoon. His own sympathies, even on a spring morning eighteen months later, were with the angry men as they prepared for the manhunt. He wondered. He had great confidence in his father, but his sense of justice was hard put to accept the fact that Travis Burdow had been allowed to escape the consequences of his drunken crime. It occurred to him that he felt the same way toward his father as he did toward Abraham Lincoln—why should the President waver so long? Why should he refuse, week after week, to start the great explosion which the young men wanted to get started and have finished before the year was well into the summer? Jethro had to admit to himself an uncomfortable feeling of anger for both the President and his father; they had not shown the hard, unyielding attitude that he admired in the talk of Tom and Eb and their friends.

He sighed suddenly and deeply at his perplexities. Ellen noticed the sigh and glanced at him quickly.

"Be you spent, Jethro?"

He shook his head. "No, I'm doin' tol'able. I was jest thinkin' about things."

"What kind of things, Son?"

"Fer one thing I was wonderin' why Abe Lincoln can't make up his mind about war. I wonder—is he like Pa? Is he so aginst hevin' blood on people's hands that he's afeared to start a war?"

Ellen stopped her work and stood for a moment without speaking, her rough brown hands resting on the handle of the hoe.

"He's like a man standin' where two roads meet, Jeth," she said finally, "and one road is as dark and fearsome as the other; there ain't a choice between the two, and yet a choice has to be made." She shook her head. "May the Lord help him," she whispered. "May the Lord guide his hand."

The sounds of morning were all around them as they stood silently in the middle of the furrow. From the fields across the creek came the monotonous shout to the field horses; up at the house Jenny's voice came clearly, pleasant as the sound of a little bell ringing.

"Here chick," she called, "here chick, chick, chick, chick, chick—"

Ellen slowly reached out with her hoe and broke a clod of dirt into crumbling fragments.

"Well, we got plantin' to do, Jeth," she said at last, and they went on with their work.

When the sun was directly above their heads, Ellen leaned her hoe against the fence, and she and the boy trudged slowly up along the fencerow toward the house. Hunger pangs twisted Jethro's insides, and he was tired, but the prospect of dinner and an hour of cool rest under the trees in the dooryard cheered him to the point where he could whistle a little and make lazy gestures of play with the shepherd dog that came bounding down the path to greet him.

The cabin they approached was small and squat, built of logs and entirely plain, a typical pioneer's cabin. Its basic ugliness was softened by a thick growth of vines clambering over the walls and roof and by a general air of neatness and pleasant dignity in the dooryard, the hedgerow of lilacs, and the prim, green rows of vegetables in the garden. Two rooms of the cabin faced west, both opening onto an uncovered porch where a half dozen split-bottomed chairs were ranged for the comfort of those who wished to rest and get a breath of air after meals, or to sit in the coolness of a spring night and watch the shadows move in over the prairies. Behind these rooms a kitchen extended the width of the house, with doors at either end opening onto the dooryard. Here huge silver poplars towered above the cabin, their roots extending like giant claws, making the ground rough and robbing it of grass. A low picket fence covered with a tangle of sweet honeysuckle stretched along the front of the yard; beyond this fence were the hitching posts in an area covered by sweet clover and an acrid-smelling little flower that Jethro knew as "dog fennel."

The road in front of the house ran due north through that line where the last glacier had melted in some distant age and left its final load of drift, a line that separated the rich, black loam culture of northern Illinois from the poor, hard-packed clay culture to the south.

Jethro regretted the melting of that glacier; if it could have hung on another hundred miles, life might have been very different for him and his family. But then it hadn't, and anyway he loved the dog fennel and the silver poplars and the hedge of lilacs on the south that separated Jenny's well-drained kitchen garden from the dooryard. He doubted that there were such wooded hills or winding creeks in the cornbelt of the north as one could find by the dozens in the clay lands, and he could not imagine contentment in any spot other than this one, which his father had chosen thirty years before. But it was a pity about the glacier. Only another hundred miles!

Jenny had poured fresh water into a big basin so that her mother and Jethro could cool their faces and wash the dirt and grime from their hands.

"Nancy and the little tykes are here," she called to Ellen. "We got a nice meal fixed fer you."

Jenny had swept her shining black hair high upon her head because of the heat in the kitchen where the food was prepared over an open fireplace, and little drops of sweat stood out under her eyes and over a very firm chin. She grinned at Jethro and whacked him briskly on the seat as he came up to the kitchen well.

"I've got a crock of lettuce fer you, Jeth, though I'm terr'ble wasteful in pickin' it too young. But I know how you been dreamin' green things as fur back as last December. Nancy and I allowed maybe yore body had need of spring eatin'."

Green food. The hunger pangs grew even sharper at her words. His body did, indeed, have need of green food, if a continuous hunger for it meant that a need existed. He had felt many times during the long winter that he would have gladly exchanged all the pork in the smokehouse and all the gallons of sorghum, which he had helped to boil down, for one big crock of salad greens. He smiled at her, and Jenny understood his gratitude. It was as much as she expected; the Creighton males did not go into long speeches about such matters.

John's wife looked up from her work and smiled shyly at Jethro and her mother-in-law when they entered the kitchen.

"I invited myself up fer the day, Mis' Creighton," she said in her thin voice. The name "Mis' Creighton" was not a joke when Nancy used it; there was a reserve about the thin, quiet girl John had brought back from Kansas four years before that kept her almost a stranger to her husband's family. She was amiable but aloof to the friendly Creightons, except for an occasional gesture of fondness for Jenny and for John's favorite brother, Bill. John defended his wife earnestly to his mother.

"She was brought up by relations that treated her harsh. To draw back and say nothin' is her way of protectin' herself. You must be patient with her, Ma, like one of yore own—"

Ellen had had long schooling in patience. Now as she answered Nancy's greeting her voice was very quiet.

"You never need ary invitation to John's home, Nancy. It's yorn, too, and you'll hev welcome any day."

She seated herself beside the door and took the youngest child in her lap. Nancy went on with her work, not sullenly, but so withdrawn that Ellen wearily gave up trying to talk with her and directed all her attention to the small boy.

The men came in from the fields soon. Jethro, because he was now a field worker, was allowed to eat at the first table with his parents and elder brothers. It was a coveted honor and he accepted it with dignity, looking somewhat like a solemn dwarf as he sat between his father and Bill, his eyes wide beneath the tumble of yellow curls that clung to his forehead and the back of his neck.

Across from him were the eighteen-year-olds. Tom was a mild-faced lad who, like Jethro and Bill, had inherited the blond hair and blue eyes of his father's side of the family. Eb Carron, a nephew of Matt's, had lived with the Creightons since he had been orphaned in childhood. Jethro admired the two big boys, but he sensed their indifference toward him and kept his distance generally. He was not especially hurt by their attitude; the youngest in the family knew his place. Besides, Jenny and Bill made up for any neglect on the part of the big boys a hundred times or more.

Bill, his favorite, was a big, silent man who was considered "peculiar" in the neighborhood. In an environment where reading was not regarded highly there was something suspect about a young man who not only cared very little for hunting or wrestling and nothing at all for drinking and rampaging about the country, but who read every book he could lay his hands upon as if he prized a printed page more than the people around him. He wasn't quite held in contempt, for he had great physical strength and was a hard worker, two attributes admired by the people around him; but he was odd, and there was no doubt of that. Men had seen him stop his team in midfield to watch the flight of a line of birds, and a story went the rounds of Bill talking to his horse as if it were a person. "He talked to it gentle," the story went, "like a woman talkin' to a young 'un." He had even attended school the previous winter when work was slack, which was surely a fool thing to do unless one was interested in "breakin' up school." He had listened intently to what a young man three years his junior had to say; he had studied and done the tasks set for him by Shadrach Yale as if he were no older than Jethro. It was not a behavior pattern of which the backwoods community approved; a lot of people smirked a little when they mentioned Bill Creighton.

Jethro loved Bill far and away beyond his other brothers; his mother understood why. "He'd put his hand in the fire fer you, Jeth," she told him once, and Jethro believed her.

John, the oldest of the children left at the home place, sat at the end of the table facing his mother. He was dark like Ellen and more slender and wiry than Bill. These two brothers were very close to one another, a fact which had always been a matter of pride to Ellen, who strove to make family ties firm and secure. John was more impatient, quicker to anger than Bill, but the two of them had sought each other's companionship from childhood; there seemed to be a bond of understanding between them that had developed with the years. John's oldest son was named for this brother, and Nancy, whose aloofness toward Ellen and Matt never once gave way in the face of all their efforts, addressed John's favorite as "Brother Bill."

Jethro neither liked nor disliked John. Perhaps because of Nancy's shyness, which he interpreted as unfriendliness, the boy extended his feeling of uneasiness with her to John and the two children. He seldom went near his brother's cabin, which was only a half-mile away, and he made no move to attract or amuse the children.

Jenny moved quickly and a little breathlessly from fireplace to table, carrying dishes of meat and roasted potatoes, pitchers of milk, and great mounds of corn bread squares, still powdered with the wood ashes in which they had been baked. She was red-cheeked with pride over her efforts at providing a good dinner, and her eyes flashed a little in the direction of Tom and Eb, from whom she anticipated the usual teasing. Jethro smiled at her when she brought on the huge crock of lettuce, and Jenny saw to it that he received a generous serving before she passed it around the table.

Nancy poured steaming coffee into big mugs, and Jenny placed one beside the plate of each adult at the table. Children might have priority to a pudding or the last piece of cake, but coffee was an adult luxury, which Jethro enjoyed but dismissed with a passive acceptance of family custom that he never thought to question. On this day of the boy's graduation to "first table" honors, however, Bill took a dried crust of bread—the remains of a rarely served "white loaf"—and after soaking it in his coffee cup for a few seconds, spread it with butter and placed it on his brother's plate. Jethro nodded his thanks briefly; he did not wish to attract the attention of the others at the table to the favor.

"This meal is right good, Jenny," John remarked pleasantly. "You air a fair cook fer yore years."

"We might ha' had cake and fixin's though, if Shad had been eatin' with us," Tom said, grinning at his sister, who could hardly hold back the pleased smile that mention of the young schoolmaster elicited.

"Can't help but feel a mite sorry fer pore Shad," Eb added solemnly. "Jenny's been feedin' him so nice lately, he won't be able to say 'No' comes a leap year."

"Jenny is fur and away too young to be thinkin' about Shad or ary other young man," her father remarked quietly.

Jenny looked to the ceiling for an exasperated second as she stood behind her father's chair. She was only fourteen, it was true, but she was as tall as

Nancy and within two years as old as Ellen had been when she married Matthew Creighton. It was also true that she had her eye on Shadrach Yale, and all had been going well, too, until recently when, after a private talk with her father, the young schoolmaster had taken on a solemn and paternal attitude toward her, which Jenny found intensely annoying and unsatisfactory.

"Wonder when Shad allows to git back?" John asked after a guarded smile had been shared by the young people.

"By nine, or thereabouts, he thought," Ellen answered. "I hope we won't be too fur spent to wait up fer him."

"*I* won't," John said. "I want to see them city newspapers—" he stopped as he saw Nancy's anxious eyes on his face. He had tried to avoid talk of war as much as possible lately; the two younger boys were too eager for it, the womenfolk too ready to cry about it. And Bill, for the first time that John could remember, had reservations about a subject and seemed unwilling to discuss it with his brother.

They ate in silence after that, but there was tension in the air. Jethro, although he was concerned mostly with the goodness of the food he ate, was vaguely aware of a troubled preoccupation all about him.

He and his mother went back to the fields after they had rested for an hour or so. The afternoon was hot, and the new freckles across Jethro's shoulders were nearly lost by mid-afternoon beneath the red burn that spread over them. Ellen untied her apron and folded it across the back of his neck; that helped a little until the thongs of the potato pouch rubbed a blister on the sunburned skin, after which sweat and insects joined forces to torment him. The buoyancy of spirit and the beauty of early morning had long since given away to discomfort and the boredom of monotony. By sundown, both Ellen and Jethro dragged down the length of the field with weariness lining their faces and tugging at their bodies.

"Seems like a lot of 'taters, Mis' Creighton," Jethro said finally. He tried to smile, but the dark circles around his eyes were more convincing than his smile.

At the end of the furrow, Ellen sat down on the grass near the rail fence and reached a hand out to the boy.

"We'll set a minute, Jeth. Sunup to sundown is a long time fer either boy or woman. The plantin' won't suffer overmuch if we spell ourselves a little."

He was grateful for the rest, and, clasping his knees, he let his head fall forward, while comfort poured all through him with the relaxation of his body. He teased an ant that tried to run across a stick at his feet, blocking its way with the big toe of one foot and then the other, chuckling a little at his own mischief.

Shadows were beginning to grow long among the trees on Walnut Hill and down along the creek where the dogwood branches stood out whiter and more like ghostly clouds with the background of misty purple thickening behind them. Jethro let the ant go on its way, and sat staring at the shadows with the lonely ache that beauty sometimes brought to him. He turned once to speak to his mother, but she sat silently, her large eyes closed as she rested her head against one of the gray rails, so he said nothing, glad to prolong their rest for as long as possible. They had sat so for ten minutes or more when the sound of wheels far down the road attracted their attention. Ellen rose stiffly and leaned against the rails; Jethro stood beside her.

"It's too early fer Shad to be gittin' back from Newton," Ellen said, rubbing her eyes. "Kin you make out whose team it is, Jeth?"

"Not anybody from right around here," he answered. "Sure is a fine, high-steppin' team though."

They watched curiously as the wagon approached, the team obviously being checked as the driver saw Ellen and Jethro beside the fence. Then, as the wagon came to a stop beside them, a young man rose from the seat and swept off his hat.

"Ain't you folks up here in Illinois a mite behind with yore crops this year, Aunt Ellen?" he called, his voice suggesting laughter.

Ellen's face broke into a wide smile of recognition.

"Well, in the name of all that's good—Wilse Graham, whatever brings you up from Kaintuck at this time of year?"

She climbed over the low rails and held out her arms to the young man, who had jumped down from the wagon.

"I had some dealin's in these parts, Aunt Ellen; I figured it was worth an extry day of drivin' to see all of you. Think you kin put me and my team up fer the night?"

Jethro could see the pleasure in his mother's face. This Cousin Wilse Graham was her sister's son; his visit would mean news of the Kentucky country where Ellen had been born, and of the relatives from whom she so seldom heard. As for Jethro, delight ran up his spine. He didn't know Wilse Graham, but the man was "comp'ny"; that meant enough to set this day apart from the monotonous routine of many others.

Chapter 2

IT was nearly dark by the time all the men were in from the fields and the evening chores done. Jethro lowered a tin bucket into the well at the edge of the barnlot and hauled up clear, cold water for the thirsty horses; then, when the chores were finished, he joined the men who were washing the dust from their faces at the big iron kettle that stood at the side of the well. The two older brothers and Wilse Graham talked as they splashed in the cold water, and Jethro could sense the pleasure they felt in seeing one another again after the lapse of several years.

In the kitchen, Jenny and Nancy hurried about getting the "comp'ny supper" ready. A couple of chickens had been dressed hastily and thrown into the pot; sweet potatoes were set to bake in the hot ashes, and dried apples were cooked in a syrup of wild honey and then topped with thick cream from one of the crocks in the springhouse. Nancy made a flat cake of white flour with a sprinkling of sugar on top, and Jenny pulled tender radishes and onions from her garden to give the taste of spring to their meal.

A coal-oil lamp was lighted and placed in the middle of the table when supper was at last ready; gold light filled the kitchen, pouring from the open fireplace and from the sparkling lamp chimney. Black shadows hung in the adjoining room where the bed had been spread with Ellen's newest quilt and the pillows dressed in fresh covers in honor of the guest. Jethro was sensitive to color and contrast; the memory of the golden kitchen and the velvet shadows of the room beyond was firmly stamped in his mind.

At the table, the talk for a while was of family affairs; there had been a death of someone in Kentucky who was only a name to Jethro, but a name that brought a shadow to his mother's face; there were reports of weddings and births, of tragedies, and now and then a happy note of good fortune. Then the conversation began to turn. Slowly and inevitably the troubles of the nation began to move into the crowded little kitchen.

"Will Kaintuck go secesh, Wilse?" Matthew Creighton asked finally, his eyes on his plate.

"Maybe, Uncle Matt, maybe it will. And how will southern Illinois feel about it in case that happens?"

No one answered. Wilse took a drink of water, and then setting the glass down, twirled it a few times between his thumb and fingers.

"It will come hard fer the river states if Missouri and Kaintuck join up with the Confederacy. Ol' Mississipp' won't be the safest place fer north shippin' down to the Gulf."

"That's true, Wilse. That's in the minds of a lot of us," Matthew said quietly. Bill's eyes were fixed on the yellow light around the lamp chimney; John was studying his cousin's face.

"As fer southern Illinois," Wilse continued, "you folks air closer by a lot to the folks in Missouri and Kaintuck than you are to the bigwigs up in Chicago and northern Illinois. You're southern folks down here."

"We're from Kaintuck as you well know, Wilse; our roots air in that state. I'd say that eighty per cent of the folks in this part of the country count Missouri or Kaintuck or Tennessee as somehow bein' their own. But this separation, Wilse, it won't do. We're a union; separate, we're jest two weakened, puny pieces, each needin' the other."

"We was a weak and puny country eighty odd years ago when the great-granddaddy of us young 'uns got mixed up in a rebel's fight. Since then we've growed like weeds in the spring, and what's happened? Well, I'll tell you: a half of the country has growed rich, favored by Providence, but still jealous and fearful that the other half is apt to find good fortune too. Face it, Uncle Matt; the North has become arrogant toward the South. The high-tariff industrialists would sooner hev the South starve than give an inch that might cost them a penny."

Then Ellen's voice was heard, timid and a little tremulous; farm women didn't enter often into man-talk of politics or national affairs.

"But what about the downtrodden people, Wilse? Ain't slavery becomin' more of a festerin' hurt each year? Don't we *hev* to make a move against it?"

"Yore own Ol' Abe from this fair state of Illinois is talkin' out of both sides of his mouth—fer the time bein' anyway." Wilse brought his hand down sharply on the table. "What the South wants is the right to live as it sees fit to live without interference. And it kin live! Do you think England won't come breakin' her neck to help the South in case of war? She ain't goin' to see her looms starve fer cotton because the northern industrialists see fit to butt in on a way of life that the South has found good. Believe me, Uncle Matt; the South kin fight fer years if need be—till this boy here is a man growed with boys of his own."

Young Tom's face was red with anger, but a warning look from his mother kept him quiet. From the far end of the table, however, John's voice came, strained and a little unnatural.

"You hev hedged Ma's question, Cousin Wilse.

What about the right and wrong of one man ownin'
the body—and sometimes it looks as if the soul,
too—of another man?"

Wilse hesitated a moment, his eyes on the plate of
food, which he had barely touched during the last
few minutes.

"I'll say this to you, Cousin John," he said finally.
"I own a few slaves, and if I stood before my Maker
alongside one of 'em, I'd hev no way to justify the
fact that I was master and he was slave. But leavin'
that final reckonin' fer the time, let me ask you this:
ain't there been slavery from the beginnin' of
history? Didn't the men that we give honor to, the
men that shaped up the Constitution of our country,
didn't they recognize slavery? Did they see it as a
festerin' hurt?"

"Some of 'em did, I reckon," John answered
gravely. "I can't help but believe that some of 'em
must not ha' been comf'table with them words 'a
peculiar institution.'"

"Well then, I'll ask you this: if tomorrow every
slave in the South had his freedom and come up
North, would yore abolitionists git the crocodile
tears sloshed out of their eyes so they could take the
black man by the hand? Would they say, 'We'll see
that you git good-payin' work fitted to what you're
able to do—we'll see that you're well housed and
clothed—we want you to come to our churches and
yore children to come to our schools—why, we
danged near fergit the difference in the colors of our
skins because we air so almighty full of brotherly
love!' Would it be like that in yore northern cities,
Cousin John?"

"It ain't like that fer the masses of white people in
our northern cities—nor in the southern cities either.
And yet, there ain't a white man, lean-bellied and

hopeless as so many of them are, that would change lots with a slave belongin' to the kindest master in the South."

Then Bill spoke for the first time, his eyes still on the yellow light of the lamp.

"Slavery, I hate. But it is with us, and them that should suffer fer the evil they brought to our shores air long dead. What I want us to answer in this year of 1861 is this, John: does the trouble over slavery come because men's hearts is purer above the Mason-Dixon line? Or does slavery throw a shadder over greed and keep that greed from showin' up quite so bare and ugly?"

Wilse Graham seemed to leap at Bill's question. "You're right, Cousin Bill. It's greed, not slavery, that's stirrin' up this trouble. And as fer human goodness—men's hearts is jest as black today as in the Roman times when they nailed slaves to crosses by the hunderd and left 'em there to point up a lesson."

Matt Creighton shook his head. "Human nature ain't any better one side of a political line than on the other—we all know that—but human nature, the all-over picture of it, *is* better than it was a thousand—five hundred—even a hundred years ago. There is an awakenin' inside us of human decency and responsibility. If I didn't believe that, I wouldn't grieve fer the children I've buried; I wouldn't look for'ard to the manhood of this youngest one."

Jethro felt as if he were bursting with the tumult inside him. The thought of war had given him a secret delight only a matter of hours before; it had meant something of the same kind of joy he had known while watching the young men race their horses up and down the road past the cabin on a Sunday afternoon; or it had meant the kind of excitement that was half-terror when, in the early days of the school term, he had watched Shadrach Yale fight a local bully who was trying to break up classes. Jethro had been half beside himself as he watched the young master feint and parry and finally knock his opponent flat on the frozen ground of the schoolyard. For weeks after that Jethro had practiced secretly at punching an old horse-collar, a sack of oats, anything, even the thin air. He had felt his face grow hot with fury as he battered at his imaginary assailant, and he had felt strong and satisfied afterward as if the fight had sparked some inner reservoir of well-being. War, he had thought, must give men that same feeling of strength and fulfillment. He had sympathized with Tom and Eb, and he had been angered at his father's command for silence when they grew loud and vehement in their demands for war.

Suddenly he was deeply troubled. He groped toward an understanding of something that was far beyond the excitement of guns and shouting men; but he could not find words to define what he felt, and that lack left him in a turmoil of frustration. He wanted to weep, but one endured a lot before he disgraced himself in *that* way. He closed his eyes for a second and swayed a little on his chair.

Jenny was at his shoulder then, pouring more milk into the tin cup beside his plate, resting her hand firmly on his arm. He leaned against her for a second and was comforted.

Wilse Graham was speaking again when the din in Jethro's ears had subsided enough for him to listen.

". . . and fer every evil that you kin find fer me in the name of slavery, I'll match you an evil in the name of industrialism. The South asks only to be left alone . . ."

"Only to be left alone to carry slavery into every new territory," John interrupted harshly, "to spread the shame of this land till democracy gits to be a word that only hypocrites kin stomach."

Bill turned toward his brother. "And must they have the John Browns and the William Lloyd Garrisons and the Charles Sumners fer teachers? We're from the South, John; would we want men of their kind tellin' us how we must live?"

John did not answer. The two brothers looked at one another steadily for long seconds; it was as if they had forgotten all the others at the table and that each was searching the other's face with some pressing need. Tom and Eb squirmed uncomfortably; Wilse Graham crumbled a piece of bread.

Then Ellen spoke. Her voice was no longer tremulous; it carried the authoritative note sharpened by long years of mothering a large family.

"That will be enough, boys. There will be no more talk of war or the troubles leadin' to war at this table tonight. The rest of our meal we will eat as a fam'ly that respects one another and honors our comp'ny."

Wilse Graham touched his aunt's hand. "I ask yore pardon, Aunt Ellen. It's been days that I've looked for'ard to hevin' a meal with you, and here I've lost myself in talk that gits me worked up and loud of voice. I didn't mean fer this to happen; I didn't, and that's a fact."

She smiled at him, gentleness replacing the stern expression in her eyes. "You air as welcome here and as much loved as when you was a lad, Wilse. I know that all of us is troubled, and our feelin's air runnin' high; but fer awhile here at the table, let's steer away from hard talk."

And so the conversation veered again, awkward and constrained for a while, but it skirted all referencc to the troubles of the day. When they finished eating, they rose and went outside to sit in the dooryard where a soft brcczc gave them comfort after the heat of the kitchen.

John and Nancy gathered up their two sleepy children and started home. Out on the open road John turned to call that he'd be back later to hear what news might be in the papers Shadrach would be bringing from town.

In the kitchen, Jenny patiently turned to the work of clearing up the supper dishes. Ellen would have helped her, but Bill took his mother by the shoulders and gently pushed her toward the door.

"You go along, Mis' Creighton," he said. "Git yoreself a little rest. I'll give Jenny a hand tonight seein' that she's treated us all so fine today."

Out in the dooryard the conversation continued to be mild. Exhausted, Jethro curled up beside his father and dove into a silent world of sleep. Matt Creighton smoothed the fair hair back from the boy's forehead and, when the air took on a chill, covered him with an old jacket.

All the others in the dooryard were tired too that night. Ordinarily they would long since have been in bed, but the need to hear news of the seething storm in the East kept them awake, every ear alert for the sound of wagon wheels from the south, which might mean that Shadrach Yale was returning from the trip to town. Jenny and Bill joined the group after a while; John came back still later. Tom played softly on a mouth organ for a while, but no one had the heart to sing.

Jethro was awakened by the general confusion when Shadrach at last drove the team up in front of the yard gate. The boy struggled through a fog of weariness and sleep to go with the others and stand beside the wagon.

In the dim starlight the young master's face looked unfamiliar. Jethro shivered a little.

There were no greetings. The family and their guest waited while Shadrach climbed down from the wagon seat. He drew a long breath when he was down and handed the lines to Tom.

"The Confederates have fired on Fort Sumter, Mr. Creighton. Early Friday morning. I waited till the papers came; they're full of it."

He looked wearily from face to face. No one remembered to introduce Wilse Graham.

"What air they sayin', Shad?" Matt Creighton asked earnestly. "How did the thing come to a head?"

"The papers say that Anderson's men at Fort Sumter have been on starvation rations for several days, and that the President warned Governor Pickens of South Carolina of his intention to send provisions to them; he made it clear that it was to be only provisions. The Confederates demanded that Anderson give up the fort and all government property in it. He refused. A Southern general— Beauregard is his name—gave him an hour's warning and then opened fire on Sumter before dawn Friday morning."

"And Anderson?"

"Held out for more than thirty hours, then surrendered the fort Saturday afternoon."

"You mean—*our* man give in?" Tom exclaimed incredulously.

Shadrach passed his hand over his eyes wearily. "What else could he do? Hungry men can't hold out long; they hadn't eaten since Thursday night. More than that, the inside of the fort was in flames. They had to wrap wet cloths over their faces to keep from suffocating."

"Was—was there lots of boys bad hurt, Shad?" Ellen asked in a tight voice.

"It's hard to believe, but the papers say that no one was killed in the fighting. They say, too, that hundreds of people climbed up on rooftops to watch the fight—as if it was a circus of some kind. And when Anderson's men marched out, the spectators cheered them. Cannon shells for thirty-four hours and then cheers when it was over."

"They kin keep their cheers," Eb Carron said angrily. "I know what I'm goin' to do—I'm goin' to git into this war jest as quick as I kin make it." He glanced defiantly from his uncle to Wilse Graham, but nobody responded to him.

"There's strong feeling throughout the country," Shadrach continued. "To open fire because provisions are being brought to hungry men . . ."

"Mister, I'd like to git a word in right here." Wilse Graham's voice was strident with anger. "This is exactly what Ol' Abe's bin waitin' fer—jest exactly what he wanted. He's worked it so the Confederates would fire the first round, and he's fixed it so they fired on hungry men. Well, fine! Now he kin set back and look pious at the states that has been blowin' hot and cold." He tugged at the collar of his shirt as if it choked him. "Somebody ought to telegraph congratulations to him," he added.

Tom glanced at his mother and then leaped into the wagon to drive the tired team into the barnlot. Eb joined him hastily. The rest of the group stood for a moment without speaking, staring at one another from masklike faces. Finally Jenny walked over to Shadrach's side.

"And so now it's war fer sure, is that it, Shad?"

He hesitated. "Congress is not in session, Jenny, and only Congress can declare war. Still, Mr. Lincoln has asked for seventy-five thousand volunteers—from the militia of all the states."

"Not from seven of 'em, I'd guess," Wilse Graham muttered.

"It's war—Congress or no," Matt said slowly, ignoring his nephew's remark. He laid his hand on Jethro's shoulder, and his big fingers clutched so tightly that the boy winced.

They turned slowly and walked back into the yard. Ellen asked Jenny to find something for Shadrach to eat before he went on down to his place next to the schoolhouse. Jethro sank down on the ground, weak with fatigue and emotion; someone—he later believed it was Bill—carried him inside and laid him on his cornshuck bed.

He woke once late that night and heard some of the men still talking in the dooryard.

Chapter 3

EVERY Saturday night and Sunday afternoon was like the Fourth of July in all the little towns of southern Illinois that summer. Miles of bunting draped dozens of platforms, where speakers, by virtue of their prestige as men of property or of exceptional eloquence, found themselves called upon to fan the wrath of the people. Families packed children and picnic baskets into wagons and drove to a different town each week, where the music of brass bands and the streams of inflamed oratory made a glorious succession of holidays for people long bound to the tedium of isolation.

A handful of old veterans of the War of 1812 suddenly found themselves reassigned to the role of heroes after years of having been all but forgotten, and their quavering voices added to the din. Pretty girls in their best summer dresses begged for funds with which to equip troops, and they blushed happily at the enthusiastic cheers of the young men for whose cause they pled. The dust and heat, the emotion and noise, became almost unbearable to many; but there were always others who returned the following week, comforting their baser selves with barbecued pork and fowl, while their spirits were uplifted by words of high resolve and confidence from the speaker's platform.

They had need for reassurance late in July when word came of the first battle of the war, a battle that had, at first, much the same picnic atmosphere which characterized the rallies being held all over the country. They read a full account of the battle of Bull

Run from the Chicago newspapers—how congressmen had driven out in their carriages accompanied by hoop-skirted ladies, all apparently eager to see the spectacle of young men butchering one another; how these carriages and spectators choked the roads when the Union troops were finally turned into a confused, bewildered mob scurrying for safety.

It was hard news; many people preferred not to talk of it at all. Tom and Eb were sullen and resentful for days that their prophesies of an easy victory should so early have taken on a hollow ring. Jethro noticed that there was no more talk of taking the South "by the britches," no more confident statements of ending the whole affair in one decisive swoop. Word of a fiasco at a place in the East called Ball's Bluff came while people were still stunned by the news from Bull Run. It was too much; some people began to say the war might possibly go on for a year or longer; others acknowledged that the South may have been right when it boasted that the northern factory workers would be no match for the bronzed young outdoor men below the Mason-Dixon line.

Bill was silent throughout the turmoil that summer. He went to the rallies, often taking Jethro along; he sat in the dooryard night after night and listened as the two younger boys chafed to be off the minute they could be spared, and as John and Shadrach made their plans to leave at least by midwinter. Shadrach decided to abide by his contract to teach the winter session of school, which would be over in February; and John felt the need to wait until he could plan for the welfare of his family and to help his father with the harvest which was to provide for both families. Bill listened quietly to all the talk, and his face was troubled as he looked at first one and then another speaker; but when they paused and seemed to wait for what he had to say, he turned away with a silent aloofness that none of them dared to challenge.

In the late summer shortly after Tom and Eb left, there was news of another defeat for the North; it was closer to home this time—at Wilson's Creek in Missouri. There were boys from Illinois at Wilson's Creek, and the war for many people in Jasper County had suddenly become a sorrowful reality. It was at Wilson's Creek that the Union commander, Nathaniel Lyon, was killed; and it was here, people said, that hundreds of boys died because of General Frémont's refusal to send reinforcements to Lyon. Jethro heard both angry words against and high praise for General Frémont in the days that followed Wilson's Creek. Frémont was denounced as the general who had made Missouri a nightmare of hatred and turmoil by his self-imposed role as emancipator of slavery in that state; on the other hand, he was praised for being a dedicated and courageous man who spoke out against slavery while the timid President would not do so.

The turmoil of Missouri spilled over into southern Illinois; Sumter and Bull Run and Ball's Bluff had been far away; but Wilson's Creek and the conflicting passions of Missouri were very close to the men who gathered to talk in the Creightons' yard and to the wives and children who listened to the talk.

Jethro listened with fascination to the new names of men and places. He heard admiration voiced for a brilliant young officer named McClellan, who had been put in top command of the army in the East. He became aware of such names as Seward and Chase; he knew who Senator Sumner was and old Thad

Stevens, what such names as Wendell Phillips and Henry Ward Beecher stood for, what roles were being played by Jefferson Davis and Robert E. Lee. In later years he remembered that these names had been part of a noisy confusion for him at first; then they had slowly taken an orderly place in his mind among dozens of others as the great drama of the years unfolded.

After the two younger boys had gone, Jethro took their place in the loft with Bill at night. Sometimes he dreamed about things he'd overheard in the conversations about Wilson's Creek, and when he awoke, often at the sound of his own cries, there was always Bill sitting on the edge of the bed beside him, talking quietly and pretending that the sound of a nine-year-old boy's crying was a manly yell of pursuit and aggression.

"You yelped jest now, Jeth," Bill said on one such night. "Kind of a blood-curdlin' yelp it was. You givin' somebody what-fer in yore dreams?"

In the dark Jethro could admit his weakness. "I was scairt," he whispered. "If I'd bin awake, it wouldn't ha' seemed so bad to think about. But sleepin'—I was scairt."

"Lots of us is scairt sometimes," Bill answered. "When John and me was tykes, we used to be scairt of witch stories that old Aunt Hetty Walker used to tell us when she'd come to help Ma with the butcherin' work. You don't need to feel ashamed of bein' scairt now and then in yore dreams."

Jethro didn't answer. He lay quietly, still shaken by the terror of his nightmare. After a little silence Bill spoke again in the same quiet voice.

"I kin set and talk a spell if it will help you to fergit any ugly things that has come up in yore dreams."

"If you ain't too sleepy . . ."

"No, I ain't bin to bed yit; sleep and me ain't on good terms these nights. I've bin roamin' the fields since bedtime; there be folks that would call that a fool thing to do, but I reckon it's my way." He stooped to remove his shoes, damp with the heavy dews of pasture and field.

"Do you think better out in the fields, Bill?"

"I don't know as I do, Jeth. My thinkin' is all of a tangle, whether I'm out in the fields or in my bed or settin' out under the poplars listenin' to the others talk. Still, the sky is a blessed thing. Much as I keer fer my fam'ly, a crowded cabin chafes me; it allus has. I want stillness and space about me." In the dim light Jethro could see his brother's face turned toward him, smiling a little. "Do you have that likin' fer bein' alone too?" he asked.

"I reckon—a little. But I don't hev thoughts enough to keep me busy; after a while I need comp'ny."

Bill sighed suddenly, as if he were very tired, and leaned forward as he sat on the side of the bed, letting his head fall close to his chest. He bore a strong resemblance to his father; even Jethro noticed it as he looked at his brother's face in profile.

"I hev plenty of thoughts," he said after a while, "plenty of 'em—and all troubled ones."

"Air yore thoughts about the war, Bill?"

"About the war—yes, mostly."

"The North will fin'ly win, won't it, Bill?"

"I don't know if anybody ever 'wins' a war, Jeth. I think that the beginnin's of this war has been fanned by hate till it's a blaze now; and a blaze kin destroy him that makes it and him that the fire was set to hurt. There oughtn't to be a war, Jeth; this war ought never to ha' bin."

"But the South started it, didn't they, Bill?"

"The South and the North and the East and the West—we all started it. The old slavers of other days and the fact'ry owners of today that need high tariffs to help 'em git rich, and the cotton growers that need slave labor to help 'em git rich and the new territories and the wild talk—" He broke off suddenly and walked over to the window where a branch of a poplar tree seemed to be trying to peer inside the small, cramped room. "I hate slavery, Jeth, but I hate another slavery of people workin' their lives away in dirty fact'ries fer a wage that kin scarce keep life in 'em; I hate secession, but at the same time I can't see how a whole region kin be able to live if their way of life is all of a sudden upset; I hate talk of nullification, but at the same time I hate laws passed by Congress that favors one part of a country and hurts the other."

Jethro was awed by his brother's outburst. He knew that Bill was no longer talking to him, and he felt suddenly desolate and alone.

"Why don't you come to bed, Bill, and leave off thinkin' more about the war?"

"I kin come to bed, but the thinkin' goes right on." To Jethro's surprise he felt his brother's large rough hand close over his own with a heavy pressure, as if somehow the owner of that hand felt a desperate need to clutch at something.

"Pa and John—they air so sure. I mistrust myself, I mistrust my way of thinkin' when I see how sure they be. I want to be one with 'em, fer John and me is close and Pa is close to both of us. And yet, I git full of anger when I see how sure they be."

"Bill, don't talk about it anymore." The plea came involuntarily from Jethro's lips.

Bill nodded then, and reaching down, tucked the

quilt about Jethro's shoulders. "I hadn't ought to be sayin' these things to you, young feller. You go to sleep now. We got a stack of work cut out fer us tomorrow. We won't be talkin' about these things anymore. Fergit 'em if you kin."

Work was heavy that fall with two hands short, and there was a heaviness, too, that weighed down upon the spirits of those who worked. Jethro labored for long hours beside Bill, and both of them were grave; but no mention was ever made of the things that had been said on the night of Jethro's nightmare. And the days followed, one after another, much the same except that each was shorter as autumn grew later.

Autumn was blithely indifferent to the tumult in the land that year. Color was splashed through the woods as if it had been thrown about by some madcap wastrel who spilled out, during the weeks of one brief autumn, beauty enough to last for years. There was yellow gold, burned gold, and gold turning to brown; there were reds blending with browns, greens with grays, and solid browns shining like silk. Jethro stood on the top of Walnut Hill one warm afternoon in October and yearned over the color that was his for the moment and would be gone at the whim of the first windswept rain that came to usher in the bleak days ahead. Oak, maple, and poplar; sumac, wild-grape, and dogwood—they all smiled at him that afternoon, and they said, "What war, little boy, what war?"

He loved Walnut Hill in spite of the sadness of the place since Mary died. There had been no sadness for Jethro when only the little boys were there; these three had been imaginary playmates for him when he was younger. He had talked with them, acquainted them with family gossip, instructed them occasionally when it had seemed timely and proper for him to do so.

Once Matthew Creighton, standing concealed among the trees, had heard Jethro explaining a new slingshot to someone very real to him.

"Bill made this fer me," he was saying that day. "You 'member Bill, don't you? Of course you do. He's a pretty good ol' Bill—better'n Tom or Eb. John, he's good, but he's got a young 'un of his own, and he likes him best. Well, you want to try this slingshot once, little Nate? Sure you kin—I'll help you. Now you two other boys mind yore manners jest a minute, you'll have yore turn. . . ."

Matt had watched Jethro's whereabouts more closely after that, and the boy realized that for some reason his father did not approve of his going up to play on Walnut Hill. After Mary was there, he stayed away through his own choice. He knew that Mary was dead, and it made a great deal of difference.

On that afternoon in the autumn of '61, he made one of his rare visits to the hill, drawn to it by the beauty of the surrounding woods and perhaps by the somber mood of the times. He no longer talked to the children though; a phase of innocence had passed, which would never be recaptured.

At the foot of the hill, Crooked Creek flowed on its noisy way across the farm, spanned at a point where it was widest by a wooden bridge that had swayed threateningly for as long as Jethro could remember, but had never quite given in to total collapse. Across the creek the brown fields stretched, bounded by staggering lines of gray rail-fences. The crossed timbers supporting the rails had the look of bayonets when they were silhouetted against a twilight sky.

A line of wild geese flew southward far overhead, and Jethro stood motionless as he watched them disappear from sight. So engrossed he was with the flight of the geese that he did not hear Bill's footsteps until his brother was quite near. He caught his breath at sight of Bill's face, which was swollen and beginning to grow discolored from a deep cut and many bruises.

"What's hurt you, Bill?" he asked, his voice barely audible, for he was pretty sure he knew.

"We had a fight, Jeth, about an hour ago. We fit like two madmen, I guess."

"You and John?"

Bill's sigh was almost a moan. "Yes, me and John. Me and my brother John."

Jethro could not answer. He stared at the cut above Bill's right eye, from which blood still trickled down his cheek. Somewhere, far off in another field, a man shouted to his horses, and the shout died away in a cry that ran frightened over the brown water of the creek and into the darkening woods.

He had heard cries often that autumn, all through the countryside. They came at night, wakened him, and then lapsed into silence, leaving him in fear and perplexity. Sounds once familiar were no longer as they had seemed in other days—his father calling cattle in from the pasture, the sheep dog's bark coming through the fog, the distant creak of the pulley as Ellen drew water for her chickens—all these once familiar sounds had taken on overtones of wailing, and he seemed to hear an echo of that wailing now. He shivered and looked away from his brother's face.

Bill sat down on the ground beside him. "Did ever Ma tell you, Jeth, about when John and me was little and was goin' to school fer the first time? At night I'd git a book and I'd say to Pa, 'What air that word, Pa?' and when he would tell me, I'd turn to John, jest a scant year older, and I'd say, 'Did Pa call it right, Johnny?' Ma and Pa used to laugh at that, but they was pleased to talk about it. They was always set up at John and me bein' so close."

"I know it." Jethro's words came from a tight throat. "What made you fight, Bill?"

"Hard feelin's that have been buildin' up fer weeks, hard feelin's that fin'ly come out in hard words." He held his hand across his eyes for a minute and then spoke quickly. "I'm leavin', Jeth; it ain't that I want to, but it's that I must. The day is comin' when I've got to fight, and I won't fight fer arrogance and big money aginst the southern farmer. I won't do it. You tell Pa that. Tell him, too, that I'm takin' my brown mare—she's mine, and I hev the right. Still, it will leave him short, so you tell him that I'm leavin' money I made at the sawmill and at corn shuckin'; it's inside the cover of his Bible. You tell him to take it and buy another horse."

Jethro was crying unashamedly in the face of his grief. "Don't go, Bill. Don't do it," he begged.

"Jeth . . ."

"I don't want you to go, Bill. I don't think I kin stand it."

"Listen to me, Jeth; you're gittin to be a sizable boy. There's goin' to be a lot of things in the years ahead that you'll have to stand. There'll be things that tear you apart, but you'll have to stand 'em. You can't count on cryin' to make 'em right."

The colors were beginning to fade on Walnut Hill. A light wind bent the dried grass and weeds. Jethro felt choked with grief, but he drew a sleeve across his eyes and tried to look at his brother without further weeping.

"Where will you go, Bill?"

"To Kaintuck. I'll go to Wilse's place first. From there—I don't know."

"Will you fight fer the Rebs?"

Bill hesitated a few seconds. "I've studied this thing, Jeth, and I've hurt over it. My heart ain't in this war; I've told you that. And while I say that the right ain't all on the side of the North, I know jest as well that it ain't all on the side of the South either. But if I hev to fight, I reckon it will be fer the South."

Jethro nodded. There were things you had to endure. After a while he asked, "Air you goin' tonight, Bill?"

"Right away. I've had things packed in that holler tree fer a couple days. I've knowed that this was comin' on, but I couldn't make myself leave. Now I'm goin'. The little mare is saddled and tied down at the molasses press. I'll go as fur as Newton tonight; in the morning I'll take out early."

He got to his feet. "There's lots of things I want to say, but I reckon I best not talk." Without looking at Jethro he laid his hand on the boy's shoulder. "Git all the larnin' you kin—and take keer of yoreself, Jeth," he said and turned abruptly away.

"Take keer of yoreself, Bill," Jethro called after him.

Across the prairies, through the woods, over the brown water of the creek, there was a sound of crying. Jethro ran to a tree and hid his face. He had heard his mother say that if you watch a loved one as he leaves you for a long journey, it's like as not to be the last look at him that you'll ever have.

Chapter 4

TWICE during the month of February in 1862 the bells rang in every city and town throughout the North, and the name Ulysses S. Grant first became familiar to Jethro.

The first real victory for the North had come with the fall of Fort Henry down in Tennessee, just a few miles south of the Kentucky line.

"God bless Grant," people shouted over and over in a rising chant the day Jethro went to Newton with his father after the news of Fort Henry. Guns were fired, and people hugged one another in the streets. Here was something to make them proud, something to give them hope after the despairing stories of Bull Run and Ball's Bluff and Wilson's Creek.

Two weeks later came the news that Fort Donelson had also fallen to General Grant. Then people really went wild with joy.

"God bless old U. S. Grant," they shrieked. "Bless old Unconditional Surrender Grant." They laughed and cried, and nearly everybody thought that the war would be over in a matter of weeks.

"What do you think, Pa?" Jenny asked eagerly a few days later, as she put down the paper she had been reading aloud to the family. "Do you think it's about over?"

Matt's face was grim. "With the Army of the Potomac doin' nothin'?" he asked. "Maybe my wits ain't good; maybe I ain't got the sense to grasp what it is they're doin', but I can't see the end in sight. That general the papers had us believe was so fine— brilliant, they called him—what does he plan?

What's the matter with him?"

"General McClellan has had typhoid fever, Pa. You know how weak that left Shad. We mustn't judge him too harsh."

Matt nodded. "Maybe I misjudge the man, Jenny. God knows I hope that one of these days you kin say that yore pa was wrong about General McClellan." He reached for the week-old paper and read again the letter that was the great tonic and stimulant of the day:

> Hd Qrs. Army in the Field
> Camp near Ft. Donelson, Feb. 16th
>
> GEN S. B. BUCKNER,
> CONFED ARMY
>
> Sir: yours of this date proposing Armistice, and appointment of commissioners to settle terms of Capitulation is just received. No terms except an unconditional and immediate surrender can be accepted. I propose to move immediately upon your works.
>
> > I am, Sir: very respectfully
> > Your obt sevt.
> > U. S. Grant
> > Brig. Gen.

Matt read on farther down the page. "It says here that this General Buckner and Grant was comrades at West Point," he remarked, without lifting his eyes from the paper.

"Yes," Jethro heard his mother say softly to herself, "and my Bill and Tom was even closer than that—"

They were worried about Tom and Eb. It was likely that the two boys were with Grant's army; the fighting, especially at Donelson, had been bitter. Some of the details of the battle neither Matt nor Jenny had read aloud to Ellen.

Finally one day Ed Turner brought them a letter from Tom. Ed looked pinched with cold after his long drive, but he wouldn't stop for coffee.

"A fam'ly needs to be alone when one of these letters comes," he said in answer to Ellen's invitation. "I'd be pleased if you'd let me know what the boy has to say—later on when Matt has the time to drop over."

Jenny had gone with her father to see about some stock, and Jethro was alone in the cabin with his mother. When Ed Turner was gone, she handed the letter to Jethro.

"My hands is shakin', Son," she said. They were, indeed, but both she and the boy knew that the real reason she was forced to hand the letter over was the fact that she could not read.

The envelope was crumpled and stained, the letter written in pencil in a round, childish hand. It was probably among the first three or four letters that young Tom had ever written.

Dere Fokes:

I take pencle in hand to let you no that Eb and me is alright.

I expect you no by now how we took Fort Henry down here. Mebby I oughtnt say we took it becus it was the ironclads that done it. Old admiral Foote had what it took and he give the rebs a dressin down but some of his iron-clads got hit hard. A boy I no was on the Essex and he was burned so bad he dide when that boat got nocked out of the fite.

Us boys didnt do much fitin at Fort Henry but at Donelson I can tell you we made up fer it. We had done a foolish thing on our way to Donelson and I will rite you about it. When we was marchin tord the fort the weather was like a hot april day back home. We was feelin set-up about Fort Henry and when some of the boys got tard of carryin hevey blanket rolls they jest up and throwed em away. Then more and more of us acted like crazy fools and we throwed away hevey cotes and things to make our lodes a littel liter. As soon as we got to Donelson the wether turned cold as Billy Sideways and some of the boys that was sick or bad hurt they froze to deth in the snow. Things was awful bad with so many kilt and others froze. I felt sick when I looked at them and so I am not so proud about Donelson as mebby I ought to be. I miss yore good cookin Ma. You tell Jeth that bein a soljer aint so much.

yrs truely
Tom

Jethro noticed that his mother's face was strangely twisted when he looked up from the letter; there was a look about her as if sorrow had been frozen in her face, a look he had not seen there before—not even on the day when he had come home from Walnut Hill to tell her that Bill had left. She stared at Jethro for a time without saying a word; then she got up and went into the pantry, closing the door behind her.

Jethro sat quietly beside the fireplace. There was

no sound in the cabin except the crackling of the fire, and there was no feeling inside him except a great loneliness. He picked up Tom's letter and read it again; then he smoothed it carefully and returned it to the envelope. It seemed strange that this scrap of paper had actually come from a battlefield, that Tom's big hand had actually touched it. He tried to imagine what the ironclads looked like and how they had taken Fort Henry; how the guns must have roared in Donelson; whatever in the world had possessed Tom and the other soldiers when they threw away good winter coats and blankets.

The pantry door opened after a while, and his mother came back into the kitchen.

"Yore ma's no comp'ny fer you this afternoon, Son."

"That's no matter, Ma."

"Maybe it would be good fer you to go down and visit Shad fer a while," she suggested after a pause. "You need a mite of change."

He turned to her eagerly. "Could I, Ma?" he asked, half in disbelief that he had understood her.

"I want him to read Tom's letter," she said, taking up the envelope. "Maybe after Pa and Jenny has seen it, you could take it on to Shad."

"Sure. Sure, Ma, I'd be proud to do it fer you."

Ellen smiled wanly at his eagerness. "It's terr'ble cold, but I reckon you could stay the night with him if he's a mind to ask you; then you'd hev only one way to walk."

"You're doin' me a real big favor, Mis' Creighton."

"I allowed it would be, Jeth. Well, you and Shad hev a good visit tonight; ask him to come here for supper tomorrow. Him and little Jenny ain't got many more evenin's to be together."

The prospect of a visit with Shadrach changed the color of the world around Jeth, and he rushed to get his chores done early. He stacked a high pile of wood outside the kitchen, where it could be reached quickly during the night. Out in the barn, he threw hay down from the loft and carried buckets of corn from the crib in preparation for the evening feeding of the stock. He was still working when Jenny came out to find him shortly after she and her father returned from their work. He noticed that her eyes were heavy with tears.

"You read Tom's letter?" he asked.

She sat down on a mound of hay, and the tears started again. Jethro stood beside her without speaking.

After a while she looked up at him. "Ma says you're goin' to go up to Shad's tonight."

"Ma's hevin' him here fer supper tomorrow night so's you and him kin talk some," he said, recognizing the envy in her look.

"Ma understands. She'd let me marry Shad before he leaves, but Pa won't. He talked to me about it this afternoon. It was the same old story—'You're too young to be married, Jenny; you're jest a little girl.' Oh, Jeth, it's horrible to be so young. Why does there have to be a war to take Shad away from me before I'm of an age that Pa thinks is old enough fer marryin'?"

Jethro was sympathetic and terribly uncomfortable. He shifted from one foot to the other and touched her shoulder timidly. She put her hand over his for an instant and then got to her feet.

"I reckon I got precious little right to be cryin' over my troubles."

He knew she was thinking of Tom, away somewhere in Kentucky or Tennessee with Grant's army. They didn't speak again until they were nearly up to the kitchen door.

"I'll help you git bundled up fer yore trip," she said then, and added hurriedly, "remember to tell me everything he says, Jeth. Will you do that fer me?"

"I sure will," he answered soberly. There was a time when he would have teased her, but not that evening. There was no time for lighthearted teasing about Shadrach Yale now that the winter term of school was over.

Inside the house, she helped him pull on two pairs of heavy knitted socks, which helped to fill out the pair of Tom's old shoes he was wearing, and she buttoned a heavy sheepskin coat around him, tying the collar up around his ears with her own red woolen scarf.

Ellen drew a flat loaf of white bread from the ashes of the fireplace and wrapped it in a clean cloth.

"This will keep yore hands warm fer a part of the way, at least. It ain't much of a gift to carry, but maybe the two of you will relish a little change from corn bread. . . ."

He was patient. He knew that after a while they would let him go. There might be another adjustment of his collar, another gift for Shad, more admonitions about his "comp'ny manners," but, finally, they would let him go. And they did—finally. He had to have his coat unbuttoned at the last minute and Tom's letter pinned securely inside his shirt, but after that there seemed to be no other reason for detaining him—nothing to do but stand at the window watching as he plunged out into the cold late-afternoon for his visit.

The deep ruts in the road were frozen and glazed with ice; the wind had a clean sweep across the prairies, a sweep that sometimes seemed about to carry Jethro before it. Tears froze on his cheeks, and the cold pounded against his forehead as he trudged along, weighted by the heavy, oversized shoes and the many layers of clothing. It was bitter, but not beyond the ordinary; suffering at the mercy of the elements was accepted by Jethro as being quite as natural as the hunger for green vegetables and fresh fruit that was always with him during the winter. When one found comfort, he was grateful, but he was never such a fool as to expect a great deal of it. The hardships one endured had a purpose; his mother had been careful to make him aware of that.

The schoolhouse with the teacher's log room adjoining it stood almost a mile from the Creighton cabin. It had been customary in years past for the schoolmaster to room and board with first one family and then another throughout the district, but young Yale had protested against the lack of privacy, and Matthew Creighton had been sympathetic.

"A man has the right to the dignity of his own fireside after a day's work," he said, and he had allowed his sons and Shadrach to cut down trees from his own land for the annex.

Shadrach Yale put down an armful of wood when he saw his guest approaching and came out to the road to meet him.

"You look half frozen, Jeth," he said, and taking the boy's hand ran with him up to the log annex. "Come on inside; I'll have you thawed out in a minute or two."

Shadrach's long, narrow room was cheerful and attractive in spite of its roughness. A bright red and gold paisley cloth covered his homemade table and fell in full folds almost to the floor; there were a few braided rugs of warmly colored woolens scattered about, and on the mantel of the fireplace were candlesticks of heavy brass worn to a smooth satin finish. Opposite the fireplace were shelves made of logs split in half and nailed against the wall to hold the books which Shadrach had brought with him from college. A guitar hung on the wall at the south end of the room, and at that end, too, there was a wide bed made up with several comforters which Ellen had loaned him from her own store of bedding. A cupboard of heavy walnut put together with wooden pegs stood near the fireplace and held dishes, food, and cooking utensils. To Jethro the room seemed perfect, as beautiful as any man had a right to expect.

Shadrach helped him out of the sheepskin coat and put him in the armchair in front of the fireplace, where the flames struck at a great log and shot up in hot tongues now and then, as the fat from a roasting chicken dripped into the fire. The warmth, the smell of food and wood smoke, overpowered Jethro for a while, and he would have sat silent, drinking in content, if his obligations as a guest had not demanded more of him.

"Going to spend the night with me, Jeth?" Shadrach asked, removing the boy's heavy shoes and chafing his feet with cheerful vigor.

"Ma allowed I could if you was of a mind to ask me."

"I think she knew pretty well that I'd be of a mind to ask you."

"She sent that loaf of white bread fer our supper; it's fresh out of the ashes."

"Good. I'm glad now that I had the sense to start a chicken roasting. Fresh bread and chicken should make a pretty good meal for a couple of hungry bachelors like us, eh?"

Jethro flushed with pleasure. Shad was like that.

Hc was different. He had book learning and was almost twenty-one; still he could make a ten-year-old schoolboy feel proud as a man.

"How's—Jenny?" Shadrach asked after a time.

"She was cryin' a little. Pa's been talkin' to her about bein' too young fer—"

"Marrying me, I know." It was the schoolmaster's turn to flush, and he looked stern, as he did sometimes in the classroom.

"Ma would let her git married to you, Shad. But Pa—sometimes Pa kin be so good, and then agin, he kin be awful strict."

Shadrach stared gloomily at Jethro's foot, which he still held in his hands.

"I respect him so much," he said after a while, "and I owe him so much, but I think he's overshooting the mark when he sets himself up as knowing exactly what is right or wrong for two other people. I think he's being tyrannical and—" he stopped himself abruptly.

Jethro felt a twinge of loyalty for his father in the face of Shadrach's obvious anger.

"Of course Jenny *is* real young, Shad," he said, with the gravity of a small parson.

Shadrach raised a black eyebrow. "Thou too, Brutus?" he asked, grinning a little sourly.

Jethro did not understand the allusion, and Shadrach seemed to be in no mood for explanations.

"There wouldn't be any question about it if it weren't for this war," he said, after a moment with his own thoughts. "I'd be willing to wait years for Jenny, but when I think of leaving her, maybe for—a long time—I guess panic hits me a little."

"When do you go, Shad?"

"Next week—John and I. He'll go as far as Chicago with me; I'll go back to Philadelphia."

"Seems like I can't face up to yore goin'."

"I'm not eager for it either, Jeth, not by a long way. I've got a lot of plans for the next forty or fifty years of my life, and being a soldier is not a part of any single one of them."

"Do you hev to do it then?"

"I guess I do. There's been a long chain of events leading up to this time; the dreams of men in my generation are as insignificant as that—" he snapped his fingers sharply. "We were foolish enough to reach manhood just when the long fizzling turned into an explosion."

"Maybe—maybe it will be over soon. I know Pa don't think so, but people in Newton was sayin' that it would, and Jenny even read it in the paper."

"What is that saying of your mother's—about hope making a fool out of reason? We finally—*finally,* mind you—have a victory at Forts Henry and Donelson. Then—hooray! The end of the war is in sight for the optimists. I'm afraid not, Jeth."

The mention of Forts Henry and Donelson made Jethro remember the letter. He hastily unpinned it from the inside of his shirt and gave it to Shadrach.

"I fergot this—it's from Tom. Ma wanted you to read it."

Shadrach took the letter eagerly and held it so that it was lighted by the fire as he read. When he had finished, he folded it slowly and looked into the flames.

Jethro sat quietly watching his teacher's sober face. He thought of boys frozen under the snow at Donelson, he remembered that he had not loved Tom as he had Bill and Shadrach, and suddenly the warm, firelit room, the smell of food, the shelves of books, all wakened a feeling of guilt in his mind. He wondered if Tom had a coat and blanket; he thought of the bitter cold outside and shuddered involuntarily.

Shadrach looked up at him. "Still cold, Jeth?"

"Nothin' to speak of."

"You were thinking of the letter?"

"I guess so."

Shadrach shook his head. "It's all a brutal business. There are going to be a lot of letters—worse than this one."

"If this victory wasn't so much, Shad, why was people in Newton yellin' so and sayin', 'God bless Grant'?"

"It *was* an important victory, Jeth; don't misunderstand me. Look, I'm going to show you something. . . ." Shadrach got to his feet and brought pencil and a piece of rough paper from the bookshelves. He drew the paisley-covered table up closer to the fire and motioned Jethro to join him beside it. "Come here. We'll have a little lesson together."

He was sketching rapidly, first the outline of a block of states, then lines to represent rivers and railroads and small squares for towns. His eyes began to shine with interest in his project as he worked.

"Now, this is the Confederate line, Jeth, beginning over here in eastern Kentucky." Shadrach studied his sketch and added a row of *x*'s to represent the Confederates. "Here it comes across the Blue Grass country; then it crosses the Mississippi about here; on it stretches across Missouri and on over here into Indian Territory—a line several hundred miles long. Now, all of this is under the command of a Confederate general named Albert Sidney Johnston—you've heard of him, maybe?"

"I think I've heered Pa speak the name." Jethro

was seeing in his mind's eye gray-clad men standing side by side, forming a single line across miles of fields, hills, and rivers; grim, forbidding men except for one familiar face. He wondered if Bill could feel comfortable in that long gray line of strangers. Then he pulled himself back to Shadrach's running explanation, which accompanied his sketching.

"Here are two rivers, the Tennessee and the Cumberland. See how they run side by side and only a few miles apart as they come up toward the Ohio, and notice that they are crossed by the Confederate line. Now, over here on the Ohio our gunboats have been lying, some at the mouth of the Cumberland, some at the mouth of the Tennessee—a threat to this Confederate line, you see."

Jethro shook his head. "What if they did threaten it? Gunboats couldn't lick that long line of Rebs stretchin' across the map, could they?"

"No, but look what they could do—what, in fact, they've already done. Notice how the Cumberland dips down into Tennessee and flows past these towns—Clarksville here and Nashville here. It's from these towns that the Confederates have been getting their supplies; this line can't move far or fight our armies if it doesn't have food, guns, ammunition. These things have been coming up the river and this—" Shadrach made a small square on the line representing the Cumberland and labelled it "Donelson"—"this is the fort that the Confederates thought would be enough to keep our gunboats from controlling their supply line."

"And was it the same on the other river?"

"In a way. See, this line represents a railroad; it comes up here from Memphis and crosses the Tennessee just below Fort Henry. Supplies have been coming up here by rail, probably every day—no doubt soldiers too, as reinforcements for Johnston. Now, do you see why Grant and Admiral Foote struck at these forts?"

"Yes, I see it now." Jethro felt a great satisfaction, which came from his new understanding. He studied the map thoughtfully. "That was a wonderful thing Tom helped to do, wasn't it, Shad?"

"Yes, it was, Jeth. We needed a victory—*how* we needed one—and Tom helped to give the Confederates a big setback. Things have been going their way all these months, but not now. This victory has clinched Kentucky to the Union side; that's a big thing in itself."

"But it ain't enough. Is that what you meant a while ago, Shad?"

"Well, think for yourself, Jeth. Our armies in the West have a part of the Union's plans to carry out, just one part, and let's see what it is. Have a look at old Mississippi here. If we can control this river, we can cut the Confederacy right in two. That's not saying we can win the war out here, but it would be a big step, because any Confederate army west of the river would be just about powerless to do anything. Here in Kentucky we're in control now; Johnston's men can't get supplies, so they have to withdraw or surrender. But down here, look how the Mississippi stretches through the states of Tennessee, Mississippi, and Louisiana—all enemy territory. And think how hard the fighting was at this little place on the map called Donelson. Does this make you want to throw up your hat and say that it's all about over?"

The log in the fireplace fell apart, sending a shower of sparks up the chimney. Outside across the prairie the shadows were almost black. Jethro and young Yale were silent, a part of the great dread that spread in all directions over the land that night, a dread that all the cheers over Fort Henry and Donelson couldn't dispel; it reached from the White House to the cities and towns—north and south, to the lonely places in the farmlands, one of which was this long log room adjoining a country schoolhouse.

Finally Jethro spoke softly. "Anyway, we've got Grant. That's good, ain't it, Shad?"

"It appears so." Shadrach's tone lacked the enthusiasm Jethro would like to have heard. "It's strange," he added. "I'd have sworn that General McClellan was worth a dozen Grants, and yet, what do we have? McClellan in the East still waiting, week after week, while Grant strikes out here and strikes successfully. I wonder what the President is thinking."

Jethro had forgotten for a while the sad-eyed President, whose pictures had been in the papers only days before, above the story of his own son's death. Willie Lincoln, the eleven-year-old boy in the White House, had died that same month.

"I guess Ol' Abe has troubles over and above any of us," Jethro said, his large eyes grave with sympathy.

"Mr. Lincoln, Jeth."

He would remember the rebuke to the end of his days. He would remember, and he would feel ashamed at the memory, but still, he would wonder. People—smart people, one would suppose since they printed newspapers and drew pictures for them— many of these people spoke of the President as "the baboon," "the ugly, ignorant, backwoods Lincoln," and other names as vicious and expressive of hate. To say, "Old Abe" was not mean or vicious; people from all around called Matthew Creighton "Old Matt." They meant no disrespect. Under no circumstance would he, Jethro Creighton, show disrespect to the President.

"I think a lot of Mr. Lincoln," he stated in quiet self-defense after a while.

"I know you do, Jeth."

"Lots of people don't. I could name you people in this neighborhood that hate him like poison."

"Not only in this neighborhood—not only in the South, either. It seems that people everywhere are criticizing him. The abolitionists hate him as much as the sympathizers of the South do. People blame him for the mistakes of his generals; and they're just as bitter about his grammar, his appearance, his family." Shadrach took a poker and stirred it thoughtfully among the red coals. "I'm not wise enough to measure Mr. Lincoln, Jeth; I just don't know. But I have a feeling of confidence and faith in him that I can't always justify. Sometimes I'm angered with him as others are; sometimes I can't understand him. But somehow my faith in him always comes back."

"I wish I could see him. Sometimes I want to talk to him so bad; I want to explain to him about Bill—"

"He has to consider men by the thousands who think the way Bill does."

"Bill was jest tryin' to git at the truth, Shad. You know that."

"Yes, I know it very well, Jeth."

"But he didn't, did he? Bill *wasn't* right in his thinkin', was he?"

"He acted according to what he thought was right. Your father and John, you and I, none of us sees the 'right' as he sees it. But that doesn't make Bill all wrong. You're going to hear some harsh things said about him; but you remember, Jeth, that it took far more courage for Bill to do what he did than it does for John and me to carry out our plans next week."

Jethro studied the rough-hewn floor. "I set such great store by him," he said finally.

"I know," Shadrach answered. "So do I."

He put his hand on Jethro's knee. "We're letting ourselves get too sad, Jeth. We'd better think about supper. How's your appetite?"

"Seems like it's always in pretty fair shape."

"Well, put a couple of potatoes in that bed of coals, and I'll set out our plates and mugs. I think we'll have some of Jenny's peach preserves by way of celebration."

His host commenced preparations for their supper with a lively cheerfulness that swept Jethro away from his troubled thoughts and back to the immediate satisfactions of the evening. Shadrach had a flair for mimicry and while he cut long slices of meat from the roasted chicken, he took in turn the role of a classroom bully, an angry woman who had descended upon the school in defense of her dull son's intellectual attainments, and a pompous director of the school who, at the beginning of Shadrach's first term, had advised the young teacher before the entire school as to what was and was not acceptable in his position.

"It's larnin' we want in this here school, young feller," Shadrach drawled, glaring balefully at his delighted guest. "It's larnin' and none of yore fine-haired gimcracks."

Jethro laughed then, a clear child's laugh, freed momentarily from the heaviness of the times. He took his place at the table beside the fireplace and, swayed happily by his teacher's mood, savored the flavor of the food, the beauty of candle and firelight, the joy of close companionship.

"I'm goin' to remember this night fer a long while, Shad," he said, smiling.

Shadrach put his hand to his throat as if some constriction had suddenly tightened it, but he answered the smile.

"Sometime, when I come back, you and Jenny and I are going to have evenings like this together. We've decided that you'll live with us and go to school, maybe to one of the fine universities in the East when you're old enough."

Jethro shook his head. "I don't know how I kin learn enough to be able to go to one of those schools, Shad."

"I'm going to leave my books with you. Some of them will be too difficult for a while, but many of them you can read, and you'll grow into the others. Jenny will help you; I'm setting her the task of reading a lot of them too."

"Jenny would copy them all out with a pencil if you was to ask her to do it."

"Don't be too sure. Jenny has a mind of her own; she sees through nonsense like a flash." He sat quietly, thinking of Jenny for a while. "I hope she doesn't make up that independent mind of hers to grow to like some other fellow when I'm gone away."

"She wouldn't do that," Jethro protested angrily. "Jenny'd hev more sense than that."

"I hope so. You watch out for me, will you?"

"Of course." Both Jenny and Shad embarrassed him a little with their talk of love; he turned his eyes to the bookshelves and tried not to be too obvious in his maneuvering of the conversation. "If it wasn't fer yore leavin', I'd be real proud about keepin' yore books, Shad."

"Well, read all you can. And newspapers, Jeth— study them. I know they're a little difficult, but you're a bright boy; you can get something out of them. The accounts you read in newspapers today will fill the pages of history by the time you're a man."

When the supper dishes were out of the way, Shadrach took the guitar down from the wall, and as Jethro sang the folk songs that his mother had brought with her from the hills of Kentucky, Shadrach worked out accompaniments for them on the strings. It was something they had often done together, and Jethro loved it.

"'Seven stars are in the sky,'" he sang softly, and Shadrach nodded, pleased with the choice. It was a song without a definite beginning or end, full of distortions acquired as it passed by word of mouth from generation to generation; but it had a pleasing melody which wailed over some secret that lay under the unintelligible patter of words.

> Seven stars are in the sky,
> Six and six go equal,
> Five's the rambeau in his boat,
> Four score's an acre;
> Three is a driver,
> Two shall be the Lily o' the Day,
> Dressed in scarl't and green-o,
> The one, the one, that's left alone
> It no more shall be alone—*

It stopped, but did not end. Shadrach sang the last lines over again as if searching for a completion.

"Those words must have had a meaning to someone at some time or other," he mused.

"Ma says that old people in Kaintuck thought it was witch-talk to the Devil, talk they didn't want

Christians to understand." Jethro shifted a little uneasily. "I doubt if there's anything to it, though," he added, conscious of the look of skepticism on Shadrach's face.

"Anyway, the witch theory was always a convenient one for something they didn't understand, wasn't it?"

"You don't believe in witches at all, do you, Shad?"

"No. Not at all."

"And yet you've told me that we ain't got a right to say fer sure that a thing is true or not true 'less we kin prove we're right."

Shadrach struck a few chords on the guitar and seemed to study their harmony closely before he replied.

"You're right, Jeth. I can't offer positive proof that there are no witches. And my anger is not with people who believe that witches actually lived back in the mountains where your mother was a girl. They have a right to their belief—as I have to mine. But I'm scornful of people who are so sure of something they can't prove that they'll torture or kill anyone who is accused, the ones who would have been in a hurry to cry 'Witch' to an odd old woman if they heard that she'd been humming 'Seven Stars' on the day their best cow died."

Jethro nodded and sat quietly staring into the fire for a long time, listening to the music of the strings until his eyes grew heavy and his shoulders began to droop. Then Shadrach turned the covers of the bed back and smiled as he watched his guest burrow under the quilts and curl up into a small, relaxed spiral in one corner.

"I'm going to keep the fire going for a while, Jeth, and do a little writing. Sleep well." He stood for a minute looking down at Jethro and then went to sit at the table beside the fire, busying himself with pen and paper.

Jethro lay awake for a few minutes; snatches of conversation, flashes of things remembered from the day, raced through his mind. There was a war somewhere outside, and it was bitter cold; there was a sad-eyed President, and one should always call him Mr. Lincoln; there was Jenny, who was not too young to be in love, and Tom somewhere with Grant's army, and Bill standing in a straight, gray line that stretched across the country until it was broken at Donelson. Donelson was a square on Shad's map, and there was a long, wavy line that stood for a river. And boys had thrown away their coats and blankets before they reached Donelson; but now the fort was taken, and supplies for the Confederates could no longer be brought in either by railroad or by river. It was a fine thing that Tom had helped to do. Well, he would read Shad's books with Jenny, and he would try to understand the newspapers—Shad thought that he was bright enough. The chicken had been good—and his mother's white bread. It had been a fine meal for two bachelors. The candlelight was like pure gold, and his teacher's shadow against the wall was like a picture.

Chapter 5

ELLEN lay in her bed, limp with the agony of a headache. It always happened when the supply of coffee ran out. Given a cup of strong, hot coffee, the pain would leave her almost immediately; lacking it, her suffering mounted by the hour until the pain became almost unbearable. Schooled to believe that self-indulgence of any kind was morally unacceptable, Ellen was deeply ashamed of her dependency upon coffee. She tried brewing drinks of roasted grain or roots, but her nervous system was not deceived by a beverage that resembled coffee only in appearance. She tried stretching out her supply by making a very weak drink, but she might as well have drunk nothing; the headaches were prevented only by coffee that was black with strength.

In late March of 1862, coffee had reached the unheard of price of seventy cents a pound, and the papers predicted that it would rise even higher. Ellen was appalled at the expense.

"This need fer coffee is an evil hold on me, Matt," she told her husband on the morning after the last of the coffee grounds had been boiled until they were worthless. "I'm goin' to suffer it out. I don't want you to bring ary drop of it to me even if you git hold of some; my body's jest got to learn." She closed her eyes as the beginning pangs of her ordeal pounded at her temples.

She could eat nothing all day. Matt sat beside her, pressing hot wet cloths onto her forehead. Jenny was sober as she went about her work, and Jethro roamed about the barn and woodlot with deep trouble hounding him.

Toward evening Matt could stand it no longer. "Send the boy down to Nancy's and ask fer the loan of a little coffee," he told Jenny. "We can't let yore ma lay here like this. Send word to Nancy that some of us will go to town to fetch coffee in the mornin'."

Jethro took off down the road as soon as Jenny told him of their father's decision. He ran for a while, and the exercise helped to warm him in the damp rawness of the March evening. He was panting as he approached the little house set back in a clearing of the woods, indistinct among the shadows and the veils of fog that enveloped it.

Nancy was out at the barnyard gate watching him as he came up to the house. "Air you carryin' bad news, Jeth?"

"Jest that Ma is bad with one of her headaches. I come to ask you fer the loan of a little coffee." He put his shoulder to the heavy gate and helped her close it. "We'll pay you back tomorrow when we go to town," he added.

She hung a milk bucket on the fence post and started toward the darkened house, where the two small boys stood at a window and stared outside.

"I ain't lighted up yit," she said as they walked up the path together. "I don't like to leave a lamp burnin' when the little 'uns air alone inside. John warned me about that; he warned me always to be keerful of his boys."

In the kitchen she went immediately to her cupboard and took down a small bag of coffee.

"I don't use much of this now that John is gone. You tell yore ma that she is welcome to it, and give her my hopes that she will soon feel better."

"Seems this is the only medicine that will help

her," Jethro answered. He was shy and ill at ease with Nancy. "I thank you kindly fer the loan of it," he added.

The young children pressed close to their mother, and Jethro patted their heads awkwardly. Nancy fondled a hand of the younger one.

"You must come down with Jenny and play with 'em a little sometimes, Jeth. They're lonesome with no pa to romp with 'em; we're all lonesome hereabouts." She walked with him out to the road. "Wouldn't it be wonderful if we was to hear all of a sudden that the war was over, Jeth? Wouldn't it be pure pleasure to hev things like they used to be, with John and Bill close brothers agin, Tom and Eb carryin' on in their crazy boy ways, and Shad back a-teachin' and lookin' bashful at little Jenny?"

Jethro had never heard her talk so much as she had in the few minutes he had been there. He looked up at her face, where some of the blond hair had escaped from the dark scarf she wore and lay against her cheeks. He wanted to say something kind and cheerful; but his tongue was tied, and he could only nod his head and hope that she felt his sympathy. When he was down the road a little distance, he turned to look back; she was standing where he'd left her with the rainy wind whipping at her skirt and the ends of her scarf.

At home Jenny hurried to make a pot of steaming coffee; when it was done, Matt carried a cup of it to Ellen.

"Drink it, Mother," he told her. "Drink the coffee, and hev one hour of comfort before this day is over."

By the time the evening work was over, the coffee had worked its miracle, and Ellen got up from her bed, white and weak, but released from the pain that had tortured her all day. Jenny took a plate of warm food to her and she ate, slowly at first, then hungrily as she sat beside Matt at the fireplace. They talked together in low voices, as if they had been parted for a long while.

After a time his father called to Jethro. "Jeth, we need coffee and a passel of other things from town. Do you think you could manage the team and do some chores fer us in Newton tomorrow?"

It was fifteen miles to Newton; to cover that distance with a team, to do the chores and handle money—that was a man's job. To be trusted with it was a huge satisfaction.

"I know I kin do it, Pa. There's nothin' hard about it—jest keepin' a level head and usin' gumption."

His father smiled. "Anyway, you've got the words smooth on yore tongue. Well, you air ten now; I reckon that's old enough to take on a sizable job."

His mother's eyes were thoughtful as she looked up at him; Jethro was afraid that she might interfere, but she didn't. "I'd be proud to do it fer you, Pa," he said.

"All right. Git to yore bed then. We'll hev to be up by four to ready everything. I don't allow to call you more than once."

They loaded the wagon in cold darkness the next morning. There were canvas sacks of corn—some to be ground for home use, some sold outright to pay for the coffee and sugar, nails, axe-handle, and tobacco that Jenny had written on a list. A few chickens lay in the wagon bed, too, their feet tied together. These Jethro was to trade for calico and thread for Jenny—and mittens for himself, if there was change due him.

Ellen made him share her coffee that morning, a fragrant cup diluted with hot milk; Jenny cooked a kettle of corn-meal mush and made Jethro's portion into pudding with a little sugar, ordinarily set aside for company meals, and a covering of rich cream. It was a good breakfast, and he felt warm and confident when he went outside again to the waiting team.

Off in the early dawn, Jethro's spirits climbed with the increased tempo of his team's hoofbeats. He had fifteen miles to travel; master of his team, navigator of his route, he felt proud and exhilarated by his freedom and sense of adventure. The wind of the night before had subsided, and, though the cold was still sharp, it was more endurable. The horses liked it; they pranced a little during the first two miles, heartened by an extra-good breakfast and perhaps conscious of a light hand on the reins.

People were moving about their morning chores in barnyards or woodlots; inevitably they stood still, watching the approach of the wagon as it rattled down the road; invariably they waved a hand in greeting and stood watching for a long time after Jethro passed, as if trying to guess whose team it was and whose boy was out on the road at such an early hour.

Three miles south of Rose Hill an old man waited at the side of the road for the wagon to approach and held up his hand as a signal for Jethro to stop.

"Be you on yore way to Newton, young feller?"

"Yes, sir," Jethro answered, and added the neighborly courtesy he had often heard his father extend, "anything I kin do fer you in town?"

"Yes, there is. I want ye to bring me ary newspaper ye kin lay yore hands on." He limped out to the wagon and peered up at Jethro. "Well, now, ain't ye kind of a young striplin' to be drivin' alone down to the big town?"

"I'm ten," Jethro answered coolly.

"I reckon ye ain't mor'n that, anyway. Whose boy did ye say ye was?"

"I'm Matt Creighton's youngest boy." He wondered how many times he had made that statement.

"Matt Creighton's boy, huh? Well! Yes, I know Matt—knowed him fer a tol'able time." He laid both hands on the edge of the wagon bed. "Ye got some growed-up brothers in the war, ain't ye?"

"Yes, sir. Tom and Eb was with Grant at Donelson; we heered from Tom after the battle. Then there's my oldest brother, John; he jest enlisted last month."

"And wasn't there one of Matt's boys that jined up with the Rebs? Seems like I heered of it—"

Jethro hesitated. "We don't know fer sure. Bill left last fall. He ain't never sent us any word."

"I see." The old man smirked a little and nodded as if at his own thoughts. "Well, it's a sorry thing. Matt Creighton's a good man, too."

Jethro suddenly felt hot with anger. "You want me to pick up a newspaper fer you, do you, mister?" he asked curtly, flicking the lines a little on the horses' rumps.

"Well, yes, I do, but ye don't hev to be in sech a all-fired hurry. I want ye to tell me somethin'. Have ye heered yore folks talkin' about a battle at this place called Pea Ridge?"

"My sister and me has read considerable about it in the papers."

The old man leaned forward eagerly. "Well, look here, I want ye to tell me about it. I got a grandson under the command of some Dutchman named Sigel. Folks air tellin' me that my boy must ha' bin in this here Pea Ridge battle."

Jethro had read the account of Pea Ridge only

days before. He had copied the map printed in the paper and had learned the names of commanders on both sides, as he followed the report. Jenny had studied it with him, and together they had mastered something of an understanding of the battle; they knew that it was a task Shadrach Yale would have set for them.

"Yes, there was a general by the name of Sigel at Pea Ridge," Jethro said, forgetting his anger a little in his interest in instructing the old man. "There was lots of talk about him in the papers. His boys like him; they say 'I fights mit Sigel' like it's a thing they're proud about."

"And this Pea Ridge place—wharabouts is it, boy, do ye happen to know?"

"It's in Arkansas, only a little way from the Missouri border."

"And was it Grant that led our fellers?"

"No, sir, it was a general named Curtis. He was the big one, I think, and under him was Sigel and lots of other officers—one of 'em by the name of Jefferson Davis." Jethro laughed a little at the irony.

"And how about t'other side? It wasn't Bobby Lee as led 'em?"

"No, but there was a passel of Reb generals there; Van Dorn was one of 'em, and McCulloch, and Pike—he's the one that had a band of Indians fightin' fer him."

"Ye don't mean to say it!"

"That's what the papers said." Jethro searched his memory for more details of the newspaper accounts. "They claim that this battle clinches Missouri to our side same as Donelson clinched Kaintuck," he added.

The old man looked down at the muddy tracks made by the wagon wheels.

"I don't know if they'd write the names of boys

that got kilt or hurt and put them in the papers—
some folks say they don't—but I allow to be on the
lookout. May as well tell ye I cain't read, but I know
my own name in print, and the boy's got my name.
That's why I try to send fer a paper whenever I see
somebody drivin' into town."

"I'll bring you one fer sure."

"Boy like you able to read the war talk, huh?"

"Yes, sir, middlin' well."

"Wisht ye was around to read me the news. Little
neighbor girl comes in now and then and reads to
me. She's got a quick, sassy way o' readin'; I much
doubt that she calls all the words right." He
struggled in the depths of his pocket for a coin.
"Don't ye fergit now—Jake Roscoe's the name."

"I'll not fergit." Jethro started his team going;
when he had gone a little way, he looked back and
waved to the stooped figure at the roadside. The old
man waved back timidly.

The sun was beginning to warm the air a little as
Jethro drove on, and it brightened the muddy, brown
fields on either side of the road with something that
looked like a half-promise of spring. There was a
quality about the air which was different from that
of the day before, a freshness, almost a hint of
fragrance. It was something that gave heart to one
who hated the cold dreariness of winter.

A little distance from Roscoe's place, the route led
through a woods for a little more than two miles, and
here the sun's rays barely got through the great bare
branches that overlapped and intertwined above the
narrow road. Once when a deer dashed across the
path, Jethro was hard put to calm his frightened team;
once he caught the red flash of a foxtail as it
disappeared in the tangle of low brush under which the
last grimy remains of winter snow lay in desolate piles.

Sometimes the wagon wheels sank deep in the mud of a low, wet spot along the road; now and then a wheel passed over a stone or a stump hidden by weeds or tangled vines, and the wagon with its load tilted precariously. Jethro maintained the stoic calm of the farm-bred boy as the wagon swayed; he kept his small, hunched frame in a position of untroubled assurance, whistling a little now and then to prove to himself that his nerves wcrc as nearly ironlike as he wanted to believe they were.

A quarter of a mile beyond the woods stretch, the road led past the Burdow place. The name, so closely associated with Mary's death, was one that was never mentioned at home and was perhaps more evil to Jethro by the very fact that it was so carefully shunned. That morning as he looked at the sagging roofs of the house and barn, the general clutter of the ne'er-do-well in the barnyard, he felt a dread as if some evil lay close to the ground on its belly and peered out at him. The physical dangers of the road through the woods he could meet calmly, but his heart pounded as he looked toward the Burdow place, and he urged his team to a trot until they were well beyond it.

It was nearly eleven o'clock when he drove into Newton, the weatherbeaten old county seat lying on the cliffs above the Embarrass River. In summer, soft skies, hundreds of full-leafed trees, and the winding river combined to give the little town an air of grace, a trace of charm that surmounted the basic ugliness; on that morning in late March when Jethro drove into town, there was no beauty in Newton to soften the view of muddy streets and the stark bleakness of bare trees and unpainted, boxlike cabins. But there were people moving up and down the wooden sidewalks, smoke rising from two or three hundred chimneys, and for a boy accustomed to the loneliness of an isolated farm, the gentle bustle of the place was exciting and full of wonder.

The town was built around a square in the manner of midwestern county seats, with the jail dominating the center. This was a small log building without doors, where the occupants made their reluctant entrance by way of a trapdoor in the roof. On the four sides of the square surrounding the jail, there were two feed stores, a harness shop, two general stores, a newspaper office, and three saloons. There was a restaurant, too, where cooking was done over an iron stove instead of a fireplace; Jethro had eaten there once when he had come to town with Bill and Shadrach. It had been a wonderful experience, and he looked at the place wistfully as he passed. His father, of course, would never consider spending good money for the extravagance of eating in a restaurant, and Jenny had placed an apple in her brother's pocket together with a slice of pork between two pieces of corn bread for his noon meal. Well, one did not quarrel with the food which he was blessed to receive, but one could not help sighing a little at the good things of life with which he was not blessed.

Down on the river at the outskirts of town there was the mill, where Jethro drove first and bargained with the grain according to his father's instructions. Later, at Gardiner's general store, the chickens were weighed and exchanged for the calico and thread that Jenny wanted and mittens for himself; with the money from the corn he bought first the coffee, ten pounds of sleek, plump beans in a heavy canvas bag—then the sugar, nails, axe-handle, and tobacco. He watched Sam Gardiner bring out a can of coal oil for another customer and guard against the possibility of the oil's splashing out by fixing a lump of gumdrop candy over the spout. The waste of such precious material cut Jethro like a knife. Maybe Sam Gardiner understood the look on the boy's face; at all events he scooped up a handful of gumdrops and put them in the package with the other things.

A half dozen men sat around the fireplace at one end of the store or leaned against the counters and cracker barrels. Jethro recognized Ross Milton, the red-haired editor of the county paper. Milton was crippled with arthritis, and his face had lines of suffering in it; but Jethro noticed that his voice was crisp and decisive, and that there was an air of assurance about him that set him apart from the other men.

He was watching the editor curiously when suddenly the name "Burdow" struck his ears, and he realized that a silent, burly giant of a man on the outer edge of the circle was the father of Travis Burdow. The man looked as if he had lived in filth for a lifetime, and Jethro felt a loathing that was new to him. He tried not to look in Burdow's direction, but time and again his eyes went back, even at the cost of a great unrest inside him.

The men paid little attention to Jethro as he made his purchases; finally, though, one of them slapped the boy's leg playfully with a folded newspaper when he approached the group for one of the items on his list.

"What might yore name be, son?" he asked cheerfully.

"I'm Matt Creighton's boy—name's Jethro."

Some of the men glanced at Dave Burdow, who started slightly at the name and stared at Jethro from small, deepset eyes.

"Well, young Creighton, is yore pa in town with

you today?" the first speaker asked casually after a short silence.

"No, sir, I brought the team in by myself." Jethro cleared his throat self-consciously. "It wasn't any trouble fer me at all," he added.

Some of the men around the fire grinned broadly, and Jethro saw one of them wink at the man next to him. Dave Burdow did not grin; neither did another red-faced young man who had put his foot on the rung of a chair and now leaned forward a little, looking coldly at Jethro.

"Seein' yore pa ain't here to answer, I wonder if you'd be of a mind to tell us where yore brother Bill is these days? Some folks around here allows he's down south shootin' our boys alongside the Rebs. Is it yore understandin' that that's what he's doin'?"

"We ain't heered from Bill since he left," Jethro answered. His eyes were wide in his thin face.

"Well, now, that's a purty answer," the man sneered. "Only trouble is that it don't quite satisfy a lot of us." He turned suddenly to look across the store at Burdow. "You know, Dave, Matt Creighton talked the boys into sparin' Trav's worthless hide a couple years ago. If Bill Creighton ever shows his face around these parts agin, maybe you'll hev the chancet to talk us into sparin' *him*."

Burdow didn't look at the man; he gathered up some bags of groceries and walked out of the store stiffly, almost as if he expected a blow in the back.

The editor struggled to get his crutches under his arms. "Another shot of whiskey, Wortman, and maybe you'll have spunk enough to pick on someone who can fight back. You know that Burdow hasn't a friend in the county, so you're safe in giving him a kick. I might add that tormenting a young boy doesn't take either courage or brains."

Another man spoke up. "All right, Red, so the boy is jest a kid. I'm not fer tormentin', but I'm ready to let him know that a lot of folks around here take it pretty dim that Bill Creighton hightailed it off to the Rebs."

"Then let folks keep their quarrel with Bill. Matt has two or three sons in the Union Army. Why should he and his family suffer for Bill's action?"

"If the editor of the county paper ain't agin freedom of speech, could I jest put one more question to this young 'un?" Without waiting for a reply, the man called Wortman turned again to Jethro. "What I want to ask you is this: is yore pa good and down on Bill? Does he teach you yore brother is a skunk that deserves shootin' fer goin' aginst his country?"

Jethro felt a great weakness. He had to steady himself against the counter for a second, and when he spoke the words were the first ones that occurred to him.

"My pa don't teach me one way or the other. He knows that I think more of my brother than anybody else in the world—no matter where he is. And that's all I've got to say to you." He looked directly at the man with an anger that dissipated his weakness.

Somebody clapped, and Guy Wortman's face grew vicious. He took a step toward Jethro, but one of the men caught his arm.

"So he's a great man, is he? Reb lover or not, he's the best man you've ever knowed?" He spun furiously toward the man who held his arm. "What's the matter with you, Ben Harris? You got a Copperhead streak in you too? Folks around here are so all-fired sure that Matt Creighton is a solid citizen—well, I ask you to notice that he's not talkin' down his ornery traitor of a son to young smartaleck here."

There was a whiteness around the editor's mouth as he slapped a crumpled hat on his red head.

"There isn't trouble enough in this country for you, is there, Guy? You'd better get out and do your patriotic duty—kick up some more mob violence. That's your forte, you know; get in on any killing you can drum up, so long as your own hide is safe."

Sam Gardiner, standing behind his counter, nodded at Milton's words. His round face was troubled, and he cleared his throat several times before he spoke.

"I go along with what Red says, Guy; there ain't any great big reason that I know of why you can't jine up yoreself instead of loafin' 'round drunk in my store."

"Maybe you'd ought to keep that mouth of yorn shet a little tighter, Sam—you and Red Milton, both of you." Guy Wortman stood glaring at the storekeeper a moment and then added, "I'm gittin' out of yore store; I ain't sayin' what else I'm doin', but I'm gittin' out."

"And I'm goin' with you, Guy," one of the men said, getting to his feet. He turned belligerently when he reached the door. "I got no use fer the thievin' Burdows," he said, as if a sudden idea had to be aired before he left, "but I'll say this: Trav Burdow is a Union soldier. I don't think you'd round up a mob so easy to go agin him if it was a matter between Trav and the Creightons this year." He went outside then, close upon Wortman's heels.

The editor stood facing the other men in the store with rage in his eyes. Sam Gardiner went over and laid his hand on Milton's shoulder.

"Now calm down, Red; they ain't neither one of 'em worth shootin'—you know that. They sure ain't worth another one of them heart attacks of yorn."

He turned then to Jethro, who stood beside the counter, his body hunched together as if in an effort to make himself as inconspicuous as possible.

"I'm sorry that you've had to hear mean talk like this, son. It was bad, all around bad, but you done right to stand up fer yore brother. I might not like what Bill done, but I can't help feelin' you was right in standin' up fer him."

"Yes, sir." Jethro nodded weakly and began gathering up his bundles.

"You starting for home soon, young Creighton?" That was the editor.

"Soon as I load up and git my team watered and fed."

Milton threw himself forward between his crutches. "Come on, then. I'll have one of the boys in my office look after your team. Let's get these things put away in your wagon."

Jethro was shaking inside when he walked out of the store into the pale sunlight. The editor drew a long breath as if he were very tired, but he smiled when Jethro looked up at him.

"I wanted a chance to get better acquainted with you, Creighton. I knew Bill a little; he and young Yale used to come in and talk to me sometimes when they came to town. I liked them."

"They was good friends," Jethro said quietly. "I was real close to both of 'em."

They carried his parcels down to the wagon and stored them in the wagon bed; fifteen minutes later they were back at the newspaper office, where a young man sat reading, his feet propped up on a table before him.

"Charley, I wonder if you'd do me the favor of taking this boy's team down to the livery stable for water and feed. I'm asking him to have dinner with me."

The young man got to his feet, grinning. "Sure, Red, glad to oblige. Hear you been blowin' off at the mouth at some of the cracker-barrel heroes agin."

Milton shrugged. "Word gets around fast."

"Ben Harris was in fer a minute." The young man shook his head. "You jest ain't goin' to be happy till you git dressed up in tar and feathers, are you, Red?"

"There are some people I don't admire much, Charley."

"I've learned that—by talkin' with ye jest a little. Well," he pulled on a jacket as he spoke, "where's the team?"

"Hitched down in front of the restaurant. I count this a real favor you're doing young Creighton and me, Charley."

"Glad to help any friend of yours, Red." Charley winked at Jethro in a friendly way and went out into the street.

Jethro glanced at the editor timidly. "I brought some dinner with me, Mr. Milton. You don't need to go to the expense of buyin' me a restaurant meal."

"I know. But I don't like to eat alone, and anyway a boy who has made as long a trip as you have needs something warm in his stomach. Come on. Mrs. Hiles usually has apple pie for dessert."

The restaurant was warm and clean, full of the fragrance of roasting meat, freshly baked wheat-flour bread, and strong, rich coffee. Jethro's fears began to fade before the hunger he felt the minute they set foot inside the place. When a plump, pink-cheeked woman placed a plate heaped with meat and vegetables in front of him with a wedge of pie at one side, he couldn't find it in his heart to be irritated at the fond hand she ran across his curls.

"All the Creightons has got looks," she said, when the editor introduced Jethro. Then she slapped

Milton on the shoulder and added amiably, "I allus said you ought to hev bin a fam'ly man, Red."

"You're a very astute woman, Lily, but like most of us, you have your blind spots. What sort of life would a family of mine have with the old man in hot water three-fourths of the time?"

She nodded caustically at that and stood surveying the two of them for a moment, her hands on her wide hips.

"I guess you got somethin' there, Editor. Well, call me if yore appetites ain't satisfied," she added, walking away.

Ross Milton turned to Jethro. "Now then, young Creighton, what sort of boy are you? Can you read?"

Jethro's voice held a slight edge. "Yes, sir, I kin. Shad left his books fer my sister and me. Right now I'm readin' a history of the American Revolution."

The editor nodded briefly. "Any heroes? Any particular man who interests you most?"

Jethro thought for a minute. "Maybe it's because Shad told me so much about him—I don't know —somehow the man that interests me most is Tom Paine."

Milton's face lighted with a big smile. "Really? The writer, the man of ideas? That's good." He stirred his coffee several times and seemed to be waiting. "Well, anything else?" he asked after a time.

"I'm beginnin' to git the hang of the newspapers a little better. Me and my sister is readin' 'em together—Shad wants us to."

"Young Yale has quite a lot of influence with you, eh?"

"He was a real fine teacher."

Milton nodded. "Well, you're lucky to have had a teacher you really liked. I hated most of mine like poison when I was a boy; I think they returned the compliment, too. There was one though—old Doc Bailey—he had a wooden leg, and he used to storm around the schoolhouse like a mad elephant. Old Doc was all right, though; he was the first man who taught me to respect the King's English."

"You mean—he learned you how to talk good?"

"Well, he tried. At least he made me sensitive to a lot of the very bad English I heard all around me. When you have your skull thumped every time you say 'fit' for 'fought' and 'heered' for 'heard' you become a bit more alert, Creighton; you even grow a little critical and want to thump some skulls yourself."

Jethro was sober. "Shad kerrected us some, but I guess he had too many other things to learn us. I'd like to talk nice—the way you and him do," he added.

The editor looked at him thoughtfully. "I wrote a little book a few years ago that might help you. When we go back to the office I'll see if I can find a copy for you."

Jethro's eyes flashed with pleasure, but the editor held up a warning hand.

"Don't get your hopes up too high. This isn't a storybook or a history book, either. It's dull, very dull. I warn you that you'll have to dig to get anything out of it." He smiled wryly as he spoke. "My effort was especially for Jasper County, but it didn't exactly set Jasper on fire. In fact, it didn't even raise a smoke, although a few people have profited by it. I think maybe you and your sister may get something out of it."

Jethro flushed. He wished that he could find suitable words of appreciation, but he suddenly felt a great shyness about saying anything in the presence of this man who had actually written a book about correct speech.

They ate for a while in silence. Ross Milton was thoughtful, and Jethro was soon completely absorbed in the pleasure of oven-cooked food that seemed delicate and tempting in contrast to the coarse fare to which he was accustomed. He ate slowly, hoping that in days to come he'd be able to remember how good each mouthful had been. When he finally pushed his plate aside and attacked the apple pie, he wondered that anything so unspeakably delicious could ever have come his way.

"Enjoying your dinner?" the editor asked after a while.

"This dinner's bin a real fine treat fer me, Mr. Milton."

"That's good." Milton leaned forward in his chair a little, and Jethro had the impression that he was anxious about something. "You're starting for home as soon as we've finished eating, aren't you?"

"I allow to."

Milton hesitated a little. "That man who caused the trouble in the store a while ago lives out west of Rose Hill—that's on your road home, isn't it?"

Jethro nodded. It had been pleasant to forget that affair in the store for a while.

"He's quite capable of making trouble over this business of your brother. You must keep out of his way as much as possible."

"I know. I don't like him."

"Neither do I. He loves violence—so long as there's no danger in it for himself—the way he loves whiskey. He'd join a mob to murder his own grandmother." The editor frowned as he tapped tobacco into the bowl of his pipe. "I'm pretty sure that he can't tear himself away from the saloon until late this afternoon, so I'd like to see you get started early. Do you have any more chores to do?"

"Nothin' except to pick up a newspaper fer Mr. Roscoe."

"All right. The St. Louis papers should be up from Olney by now. We'll get one at my office."

He motioned to Mrs. Hiles, and she came over to collect for their meals. She brought another wedge of pie, in a brown bag, and handed it to Jethro.

"This is fer you in case you don't get home in time fer supper," she said. "I took it as a real compliment the way you plowed into that first piece."

At the newspaper office, Jethro picked up one of the papers while Ross Milton hunted for his book. A cartoon caught his eye; it showed an outraged McClellan falling head over heels from the top rung of a ladder marked "General-in-Chief" to a lower one labelled "Army of Potomac—Only," while a stern-faced Lincoln stood close by and dusted his hands. Here was something to tell Pa; Matt's anger against McClellan had been growing by the week. Jethro remembered Shad's words when they had talked together only a few weeks before: "I would have guessed that McClellan was worth a dozen Grants."

When the editor finally returned with the book, he extended it to Jethro with a grin.

"Here you are, Creighton; this book is yours if you can use it. We won't expect miracles, but it might just happen that you'll get some good from it."

They shook hands, and Jethro felt good as he walked down the street to the hitching post, where the young man from the newspaper office had tied his team. When he was in the seat and ready to leave, he looked back. Ross Milton, standing between his crutches in the doorway, waved to him.

The team trotted briskly out of town, across the bridge spanning the river, and on up the road between meadows that seemed to have grown a little brighter since morning. The bag of coffee was at his feet; the wedge of pie, the book, and the newspaper were placed safely on the seat beside him. He thought with satisfaction of the things he would have to tell Jenny and his parents that evening. He pushed the scene at the store to the back of his mind, but the dinner with Ross Milton, the kindness of Mrs. Hiles, the gift of a book actually written by the editor himself—these were the tidbits with which the traveler could reward his family's hours of waiting for his return.

He did not know how much he would tell about the ugly words of Guy Wortman and the others who were ready to believe that Matt Creighton was a Copperhead, because of Bill's actions. It would worry his parents, Jethro knew.

They had heard of incidents downstate: a family murdered because they were suspected of being Southern sympathizers, an abolitionist family attacked in the middle of the night and their house fired by men who hated what their victims stood for. Southern Illinois was beginning to feel the tumult that had rocked Missouri. There was a tradition of a free state in Illinois, a tradition long since established with the opening of the Northwest Territory, but it was being challenged by thousands whose ties with the South were close and of long standing.

Jasper County was predominantly Northern in its sympathies, but there were many whose loyalty was secretly with the South or was suspected of being there. Now, the Creightons were one of those families—a Copperhead family whose youngest boy spoke up for a brother who had gone South. The ones who wanted to hate, the sullen ones with pigs' eyes, and the angry ones who loved violence as they loved whiskey would not care to remember that Tom and Eb, and now John and Shad, were in the Union Army. A man in the store had said, "I don't think you'd round up a mob so easy to go against him if it was a matter between Trav Burdow and the Creightons this year."

At first the miles seemed to pass faster than they had on the trip into town, but for all that, Jethro began to grow tired after three hours or so had gone by. It had been a long time since four o'clock that morning when he had crawled out of bed at his father's first call, and the excitement of the day, as well as its length, had taken toll of his energy. He found himself nodding a little now and then as the slow creak of the wheels invited sleep, and he had to shake himself briskly and to talk aloud for a while when the monotony became overpowering.

The sun was getting low by the time he reached the ruins of what had been the county's first schoolhouse, a landmark known as the eight-mile point north of Newton. It was early twilight when he reached the Burdow place, where the wagon that Jethro had seen in front of the general store in Newton now stood in the cluttered barnlot.

Two dogs rushed out toward Jethro's team, barking shrilly and snapping at the heels of the horses. A woman came to the door of the cabin and stood, half lost in the shadows, as she looked out at the passing wagon. By twilight the place seemed even grimmer than it had that morning.

The two-mile stretch of woods road was just ahead—the hardest two miles of the trip if one considered the terrain. But to Jethro the several yards along the dooryard and barnlot of Dave Burdow's place were full of a sinister threat that made the woods road a welcome relief. When it curved among the trees and the Burdow cabin was lost to sight, he breathed easier and shifted himself stiffly on the seat as he prepared for the ordeal of mudholes and jutting tree stumps in the road ahead.

The curve, however, was no sooner rounded than Jethro discovered that the vague dread he had experienced in passing the cabin had now become a reality. A man stood among the trees at the edge of the road, a saddled horse at his side. As Jethro approached, he walked slowly out, as if he'd known the wagon would soon be along and had been waiting. Jethro saw that it was Dave Burdow.

With a curt gesture, he motioned Jethro to stop. "Like to ride with ye a piece," he muttered, and climbed over the wheel and into the seat without raising his eyes to the boy's face. He led his own horse by a strap.

Jethro shrank from the great bulk beside him with fear and revulsion. He did not dare look at Burdow, but he remembered the sullen, piglike eyes that had stared at him in the store that morning. He remembered, too, hearing usually mild Ed Turner speak in loud anger about Dave Burdow a few weeks after Mary's death.

"Decency ain't in him," Ed had declared. "He's had nary a word of human feelin' fer what happened to that little girl, nary a word of thanks that Matt saved his worthless boy from his neighbors. He's more of a dumb brute than a man."

Dave Burdow was as silent as the darkness that was drawing in around them. There was no sound but the creaking of the wagon as it floundered through the sour-smelling mud and over mammoth tree roots. The air held a damp chill, as if the sun that had given a pale, late-winter brightness to the streets in Newton had been too weak to penetrate the dense branches above the woods road. The team was tired, the going slow, and a quarter of a mile was covered in only something less than an eternity.

Jethro did not actually visualize the grim possibilities that faced him. He was still too much a child, still insufficiently acquainted with violence, to believe that bodily harm could possibly come to him. Ugly things happened, it was true, but to people who were distant, unknown people—not to someone named Jethro Creighton. He was afraid, but his fear was vague, and anger was as strong as fear when he thought of the precious bag of coffee and of the little gifts—gifts were as rare for him as comforts or luxuries—the book, the wedge of pie, the handful of Sam Gardiner's candy. There was the team, too, and the wagon. If a thieving Burdow took these, what could a boy who had been trusted with them say to his father? "You jest hev to keep a level head and use gumption," he had said confidently the night before.

He tried to hold himself firm, but after a while the strain became too great, and a shudder shook his body with sudden violence. The silent man at his side turned then and looked at him for the first time.

"Ye got no call to be afeared," he said roughly. "I ain't aimin' to hurt ye none."

Jethro didn't answer, and they drove on in silence again for so long that he was startled when Dave Burdow spoke again. His voice was less rough this time, and it held a resonance of anger and sadness that made Jethro remember the stories he had heard of mad old John Brown.

"There be things that's evil in these woods tonight. I seed evil apassin' my place a while ago, comin' in from the short-cut road to town and reelin' in the saddle. I heered evil braggin' in the saloon today about layin' fer a young 'un on his way home." He reached over and took the reins from Jethro's hands. "I'd best drive till we're out of the brush," he added. "We're gittin' close to the place where some piz'nous snake might strike quick."

The world was turning upside down for Jethro. He felt as if he were someone else, someone looking from far off at a boy who had started from home with a team and wagon on a March morning that was at least a hundred years ago. When he tried to speak he found that his voice, like his identity, had gone too; his lips worked as they had often seemed to work in a bad dream to form the words he wanted to say, but no sound passed them, and there was nothing to do but sit quietly while his mind floundered in the uncertainties that beset it.

At a point near the north end of the woods road there was a bridge spanning the ravine that cut a deep, jagged gash across the road and through the fields beyond. As they approached the bridge, Jethro saw the dim outline of a horse beside a tree; Dave Burdow saw it too, and he leaned forward in the seat, his hands tightening on the lines and the strap by which he led his own horse beside the wagon.

At the bridge the thing happened quickly and was over without a word being spoken by either the attacker or the attacked. A man leaped up from the ravine when the wagon was midway across the bridge and, running up beside the team, laid a long whip across the backs of the horses. There was a bad moment as the horses plunged and kicked and as Burdow's horse responded to the fright of the team; seconds later the tethered horse at the roadside broke away and galloped off into the darkness ahead of the wagon.

The thing was over quickly with Dave Burdow's strong hands on the reins. It had been a close brush with tragedy, but as the horses became quiet again the event became as routine in Jethro's mind as the tilting of the wagon had been that morning; it would be a while before he would grasp the full terror of the thing that had happened.

There was no word between the two in the wagon when the danger was over. Both man and boy seemed to be in tacit agreement that the attack at the bridge was a closed incident, a thing for which they felt a solid indifference. Jethro realized that he had clung to Dave Burdow's arm during the worst of the moment, and he drew aside.

Shortly after the incident at the bridge, the light from Jake Roscoe's cabin could be seen through the trees. The old man was waiting at his gate when the wagon finally came up. "Air ye young Creighton?" he called out. "Did ye bring me my paper?"

Burdow stopped the team, and Jethro handed the paper down across the wheel. He found that his lips were still too numb for speech, and he wanted desperately to be beyond earshot of the old man's plaintive questioning.

"Who is it that's with ye?" Roscoe asked, peering up through the darkness.

Jethro could only shake his head, and Dave Burdow did not speak. The team started on, no less communicative than the two figures in the wagon, and the old man was left muttering angrily at his gate.

A little distance beyond Roscoe's place, Dave Burdow stopped the team again and prepared to climb down from the wagon.

"Wortman caint foller ye—ye can git on by yoreself now." He jumped from the top of the wheel to the ground and turned his horse's head to the south.

Jethro managed the words "I'm obleeged," but Dave Burdow made no sign of having heard him. He mounted his horse and, without looking around, started back over the road they had just traveled.

Jethro watched horse and rider for as long as he could see them; then he flipped the lines across the backs of his team. There were still four full miles to cover, and he was weak with a deep weariness that seemed to penetrate every muscle of his body. His head swam in a way that frightened him, and to protect himself against the danger of falling off the high seat, he slid down into the bed of the wagon and leaned against the side. The horses needed no guiding now; they knew they were on the last lap of the day's journey.

There was a dim new moon, which he hadn't seen while he was in the woods, and Jethro watched it dully as home came closer, step by step. His thoughts skirted the danger that had threatened him; he wondered instead if Guy Wortman's horse had run away for good and all; he wondered, too, what Dave Burdow would say to the woman who had watched Jethro from the shadowy door of her cabin. Then he slept a little and wakened suddenly to feel about the seat and bed, locating each parcel that he had brought with him from town.

When at last he saw the light from the kitchen window at home, he urged the horses to a trot, and under cover of the wagon's rattling, the sound of a few sobs amounted to almost nothing. A long rectangle of light appeared in the dark outline of the cabin while he was still some distance down the road; he knew then that his approach had been heard, that the door was opened, and that someone was coming outside to welcome him.

At home, the relief of those who had waited was obvious in the excitement of their welcome. When the parcels were carried inside and the team cared for, Jethro sat beside his father at the table, with Jenny and Ellen facing him and waiting for all the news of his trip to town. They noticed his pallor, and Ellen's eyes were tender as she recognized the signs of tears, but they would not shame him by asking if the trip had been too hard for him. They spoke instead of his purchases; he'd shown good judgment in the things he'd bought. They congratulated him on being able to account for every penny of the money earned through sales and expended for their needs.

Jethro chose carefully from among the day's happenings those things that he wished to tell them. He related parts of his conversation with old Jake Roscoe; he told them of meeting the editor in Sam Gardiner's store and that the young man named Charley had looked after the team while Jethro had gone to the restaurant for dinner with Mr. Milton. He made them taste Mrs. Hile's pie and share Sam Gardiner's candy; he showed them the book on English usage and told them about the cartoon in the paper relating to General McClellan's late demotion. He spoke slowly and a little wearily, but they were too much interested to guess that he was holding back some news of keener interest.

After a while, Ellen held out her hand to him. "You air spent, Jethro; I kin see it in yore face. Let's all git to our beds and talk the rest of yore trip in the mornin'."

Jenny pushed her chair back and Matt started to rise, but Jethro sat in his place and motioned toward the others to sit again.

"There is more I hev to tell you before we sleep," he said. There was a catch in his voice, and they all looked at him with anxious eyes. Then he stretched his arms out on the table and, with a long sigh, began his story.

"I didn't tell you this, but in the store this mornin' there was a man named Guy Wortman. And there was another man, Trav Burdow's pa—"

Chapter 6

MATT did not sleep the night after Jethro's return from Newton, and the next morning he was up at dawn moving aimlessly about the cabin and out around the dooryard and woodlot. Ellen had managed to sleep a little in the early morning hours, but she got up when she heard him and prepared a breakfast that neither of them wanted. They drank a little coffee and looked at one another in silence; she noticed that his face was pale, but so was the dim light in the cabin and so, she supposed, was her own face. A moment later, though, a frown came between her eyes as she watched his trembling hand place his cup back in its saucer.

"You air ailin', Matt," she said quietly. "Why don't you git back to bed and rest a little? There ain't so much that needs doin' this mornin'."

He shook his head. "If you ask me am I afeared, the answer is 'yes'; ailin', it's 'no.'" He pushed his chair back from the table a little. "I think I'll go over and ask Turner to drive to Newton with me this mornin'. I want to talk to him and to some of the men down there as knows this Wortman."

"Will you stop at Burdow's, Matt?" she asked tensely.

His fingers clutched at strands of his beard as if it were necessary to hold on to something. "You'd hev me do it, wouldn't you?"

She nodded. "We've held it aginst him that his boy stuck a knife in our hearts; now he's grabbed a second knife that was aimed at us."

"Mother," he turned toward her with eyes full of

despair, "if you could ha' knowed back in 1830 of all the griefs you'd hev . . ."

She put a hand out to him quickly when he paused. "Yore spirit needs bolsterin' today, old man." She smiled at him. "You know good and well I wouldn't ha' believed ary prophecy. And if I had, I reckon I'd ha' risked it. I wanted Matt Creighton fer mine awful bad, if you air of a mind to remember."

They were silent again, each of them preoccupied and troubled. Upstairs they heard Jenny in her room getting dressed to come down to the kitchen; there was no sound from Jethro's room.

"Let the boy sleep," Matt said after a minute. "Yesterday was too much fer a lad of his years."

"I'm glad that you air willin'," she answered. "I don't want to be a soft mother because he's my last, but it would hurt me to deny him his rest this mornin'."

They got to their feet, and Ellen began to gather up their cups and saucers while Matt pulled on his jacket and cap. "I aim to walk over to Ed's now," he said, and she nodded absently.

A minute or two later she thought she heard a noise at the gate, and hurrying out, she found him lying unconscious on the ground with one hand clutching at his left side.

She covered him with heavy comforters while Jenny ran to Ed Turner's for help. Then, between them, they got Matt to his bed while the Turners' oldest boy drove over to Hidalgo for the doctor.

Matt revived, but the vigorous, erect Matt Creighton was gone. A man who looked twenty years older had taken his place.

If someone had asked Jethro to name a time when he left childhood behind him, he might have named that last week of March in 1862. He had learned a great deal about men and their unpredictable behavior the day he drove alone to Newton; now he was to learn what it meant to be the man of a family at ten. He had worked since he could remember, but his work had been done at the side of some older member of the family; when he had grown tired, he was encouraged to rest or sometimes he was dismissed from the task altogether. Now he was to know labor from dawn till sunset; he was to learn what it meant to scan the skies for rain while corn burned in the fields, or to see a heavy rainstorm lash grain from full, strong wheat stalks, or to know that hay, desperately needed for winter feeding, lay rotting in a wet quagmire of a field.

By the second week of April that year, the fields were dry enough for plowing, and Jethro, full of the optimism of inexperience, harnessed his team and went out to the field alone. Ed Turner, driving past on his way home from town, stopped and waited until Jethro could get from mid-field up to the fencerow.

"You kin count on me fer whatever help I kin spare, Jeth, and whatever counsel. You air young fer what's ahead—and I don't like to see a boy made a man too soon. I reckon, though, that it was writ you'd be the staff of yore pa's old age."

Jethro flushed, proud and embarrassed at the same time. "I reckon I kin manage," he said in his slow way.

Ed hesitated and then pointed to the newspaper on the seat beside him. "There's bin a bad fight, Jeth, down in south Tennessee."

"Grant's army?" Jethro asked quickly.

Ed nodded. "At a place they call Pittsburg Landing—somewhere down on the Tennessee River. Grant let hisself git su'prised by the Rebs—papers say that it was Sherman and Buell as saved things. They say it was a vic'try fer us, but they're down on Grant—make it sound like he's next of kin to Jeff Davis."

"Two months ago they was yellin' and praisin' him to the skies after Donelson."

"I know. It's a sight easier to be a general in a newspaper office, I reckon, than it is to be one out on a battlefield. I'm not losin' my feelin' fer ol' Grant—not yit, I ain't."

"The fightin'—it was bad, was it?"

Ed understood his meaning. "Upwards of twenty thousand, Jeth; mor'n twelve thousand of 'em was our boys."

Jethro looked up at the neighbor thoughtfully. "I reckon we'd best not tell Pa—not till we hear from Tom or Eb."

"It would be better that way," Turner agreed. "You and Jenny kin read the papers off to yoreselves somewhere; don't talk about it before yore pa—or yore ma either, fer that matter."

"Pa don't ask about the news these days—that's one way he's so diff'rent." Jethro was troubled. "How long do you think it might take a letter to git up from Tennessee?" he asked after a while.

"It's bound to take a spell. I wouldn't worry, was I you. You'll be hearin' from young Tom or Eb before long. Remember the fight at Donelson was a bad one too, and both the boys come through without a scratch. I don't doubt but what you'll hev a letter one of these days."

"Sure hope so." Jethro turned slowly back toward his team, his thin shoulders stooped a little. He did not weigh more than eighty pounds. Ed Turner must have been sharply aware of the look of frailty about the boy in contrast to the great plow horses and the wide fields where Matt with his four boys and Shadrach Yale had worked only the year before. His eyes were troubled as he made ready to drive on.

"Now, spell yoreself every hour or so, Jeth—don't drive too hard. I'm goin' to send one of my boys over to help you before long, and some of the men over tow'rd Hidalgo, they 'low to give you a day's work now and agin—yore pa's got plenty friends around here in spite of all the Wortmans and their kind in the county."

One afternoon later in the week Jenny had hurried with her housework and was prepared to go back to the field with her brother.

"One of us kin take a furrow or so while the other one rests; we'll save each other a sight of weary achin' by day's end," she told her mother.

Ellen nodded without speaking. She watched them as they walked off to the field together, and then turned slowly back to sit beside her husband.

"They're good young 'uns, Matt," she said.

He cried very easily in his weakness. "I bin thinkin' of young Tom," he said after a moment.

"I know. I think of him too—him and all the others. We'll be hearin' from some of 'em soon. You're not to fret, Matt; we mustn't give trouble a shape before it throws its shadder."

He closed his eyes and did not answer. He was suddenly old and weak—not himself anymore, but rational enough to know that several troubles had already thrown their shadows.

Out in the field Jethro and his sister were able to escape for a while from the gloom of the cabin. April was in full bloom, and they were young enough to accept the sunlight and color of a new spring as omens of good fortune. They liked being together, and in the early afternoon before he grew too tired, Jethro would walk along with Jenny when she took her turn at the plow, preferring conversation to solitary rest.

"I can't quite see how they're callin' it a vict'ry," he said, his eyes fixed on the ground as they walked along the furrow. "If we'd got down to Corinth and pushed the Rebs out, that would hev bin good news. This way, looks to me like all we done was to keep the Rebs from hevin' a vict'ry."

"Anyway, we held on, Jeth. They can't say that our boys was puny alongside of theirs—like they said about us last year at Bull Run."

"What I wonder about though, Jenny, is why Grant wouldn't ha' knowed that the Rebs was fixin' to attack. I think about it over and over—why didn't he be more keerful?"

"Air you goin' aginst Grant like all the papers, Jeth?"

"No, I ain't. Things went aginst him—Buell was late in gittin' more soldiers to him—that Wallace feller got himself lost in the woods right when Grant needed him bad. If things had happened a little different, maybe the papers would be singin' a different tune about Grant."

"They're sayin' now that the President ought to fire him."

"I wonder why it is that folks air so ready to be down on Grant—even Shad wasn't exactly fer him the way most folks was after Donelson—"

"I don't doubt that it's because of that awful name—Ulysses. You know the name I like, Jeth? Don Carlos Buell. If ever I have a little boy, I aim to name him Don Carlos."

Jethro looked at her with mingled astonishment and disapproval. "Jenny, sometimes you air so foolish I'm su'prised that Shad ever took a likin' to you."

Jenny produced deep dimples in her hot cheeks. "You and Shad air much alike, Jeth—too sober and solemn fer yore own good. Sometimes you make me think you air a little ol' man with a boy's body. You and Shad—both of you need a foolish girl around to jolt the corners of yore mouths into a grin once in a while."

He was pleased to be compared with Shad, and he walked for a while in silence as he thought it over. Then Jenny spoke again, and he was surprised at the change in her voice.

"I'm thinkin' about the battle too, Jeth—and the boys—and maybe Bill on the other side. There's lots of thoughts deep inside me; I ain't jest as foolish as I seem sometimes."

"I know it," he said gruffly.

They worked together often during the following weeks. Ed Turner's oldest boy came over to help every few days, and during one week three men from neighboring farms came over and put in a day's work. Jethro appreciated their help, but he was always glad when it was Jenny who went with him to the field and talked of one thing and another and sometimes made him laugh. The difference in their ages seemed to have narrowed that spring, and subtly he stepped out of the role of a petted little brother and became a peer of Jenny, with the full rights of teasing or criticizing that had belonged to Tom a year ago.

But Jethro was to experience one attack of childish fury before the transition to his new standing was fully accomplished. It happened with the arrival of a letter from Shadrach Yale, and it was very painful.

The day had been, up until the noon hour, one of more optimism than they had known that month. Matt was much better, well enough to come to the table that noon and to listen with interest as Jenny and Jethro told him about the progress of the farm work. Ellen's face was full of relief, and she had stopped long enough in the midst of washing, cooking, and weeding her garden to gather a bunch of lilacs from the hedge and to place them in a small stone jar at Matt's plate.

Jenny and Jethro were cheerful as they made their plans for the afternoon: she, with the help of Ed Turner, would finish the planting in the field south of Walnut Hill; Jethro would go on with the plowing down at John's place by himself. They ate with the hearty appetites of youth and health and accepted with satisfaction the few quiet words of praise that Matt had for them. That praise in itself was something new; Matt had always demanded hard work from his children—it was a duty imposed upon them by necessity and by a pioneer philosophy—and praise was neither given nor expected; now the necessity was greater than ever, but a changed man imposed the labor. The older children of the family would have been surprised and, according to their several natures, pleased or outraged by their father's consideration of these two younger ones.

Israel Thomas brought the letter from Hidalgo while the family still sat at the table. Jethro ran out to the road to take it, to report his father's improvement and the state of the farm work in general. Israel handed the letter over with a marked lack of enthusiasm.

"Hoped I'd be bringin' yore pa a letter from young Tom," he said sourly. "This here is prob'ly nothin' more than some sweet talk fer Jenny from the schoolmaster. Well, here 'tis—tell 'er not to b'lieve mor'n half of what is writ in it."

Jethro took the letter inside and handed it to Jenny with a big smile. It was addressed to her, of course, but that didn't matter; he settled down happily to wait his turn at reading it.

There had been other letters from Shadrach since he left in February, but as if determined to obey Matt's ultimatum of "no romance" with fifteen-year-old Jenny, the young soldier had addressed himself to the entire family. Spring, however, had reached a training camp outside Philadelphia, and it was as soft and gentle as the spring that had settled over southern Illinois; perhaps some mood of defiance for his future father-in-law had welled up in the heart of a lonely boy—at all events, this was a love letter, and it was all for Jenny.

When his sister left the table and ran off to her room with the letter, Jethro was irritated, but tolerant of her rights; however, when she returned, with flaming cheeks, and began to read a few excerpts from the closely written pages, he was dismayed. He wanted to study every line, every flourish of the beloved hand; he wanted desperately to know every word that had been traced by Shadrach's pen.

Letters were so few, and on every other occasion that Jethro could remember, any letter received by one member of the family had been read and discussed by every other member. That was courtesy, common decency—whatever one wished to call it. And now came this one, as precious a letter as had ever been received, and there was Jenny reading a line here and there, pausing to blush and most obviously skip over an entire paragraph, sometimes flipping over a whole page without sharing a single word.

". . . Tell Jeth I take great pride and pleasure in hearing of his study of the newspapers. . . ." Blushes and a sudden stop. Then again, *"When I remember the long hours of my illness with typhoid, and the loving care with which your mother watched over me, I feel that I do, indeed, have a mother who replaces the one I lost as a child. And it is my fervent hope, dear Jenny—"*

It was soon evident that she was not going to read Shadrach's fervent hope aloud, and Jethro, full of hot anger toward her, was amazed that his parents were tranquil and undisturbed. They even glanced at one another and smiled a little. Jethro had no smiles—not in his heart or mind or on his lips.

"I would as soon eat somethin' wonderful good in front of her and jest offer her a crumb," he thought bitterly.

He set his lips firmly together and got out of the room as soon as possible. It helped a little to have hard work facing him; he harnessed his team and rode away toward John's place without glancing back to wave good-bye to Jenny. He was in no mood to be gracious to anyone, much less to Jenny.

His rage stayed with him for a while as he walked behind the horses, back and forth along the length of the field.

"She ain't never bin selfish before," he thought, as he rehearsed Jenny's fall from his favor. Then remembering a lesson from Ross Milton's book, which he and Jenny had been studying together when they had a little time, he tried fitting his angry thoughts into better English. "She's never been selfish before," he amended, and some of his anger was dissipated before the satisfaction of his new learning.

In the middle of the afternoon, Nancy came down to the field with her children and waited for Jethro in the shade of a big oak tree just inside the fencerow.

"We brought you a little somethin' to lighten yore work, Jeth," she said in her quiet way. She held in one hand a slice of freshly baked white bread spread with butter and in the other a stone jug filled with cold milk.

He threw the lines over a post and sat down in the shade of the tree. The children came and sat close to him; he had paid more attention to them lately, knowing that it pleased Nancy, and they had grown fond of him.

"They take you fer a man full growed, Jeth," Nancy said, smiling. "I wouldn't doubt but what they sense somethin' of John about you."

He took a long, appreciative drink from the milk jug. "This is real nice, Nancy," he said, wiping his mouth and nodding to her. He was more at ease with her lately; she was beginning to seem more like one of the family.

Her eyes were big in her thin face. "Has there bin any letter up at yore place, Jeth?"

"Jest one—from Shad. Nobody gits to read it 'cept Jenny." His voice was curt.

Nancy watched his face thoughtfully. "He's still in trainin', I reckon. Him nor John wouldn't be in the fightin' yet, would they?"

"No, it's too soon. It takes a spell to git the hang of soldierin', I guess."

He offered a bite of bread and butter to each of the children. It would be just as pleasing to him, he thought, if she questioned him no further about Shad's letter.

He ate the rest of the white bread soberly and watched his two young nephews run a little way down the furrow, their small white feet pretty against the brown waves of freshly plowed earth that lay sleek and glistening in the sunlight. It was April again. April. Jethro liked the sound of the word. He thought how beautiful it would sound in poetry.

"Did ever you think how nice the word April sounds, Nancy?" he asked after a while.

She smiled a little. "It does hev a nice sound, Jeth. April's allus bin my month, the month of my bornin', the month of my marryin'. But now—" she sighed and turned toward Jethro earnestly. "In yore studyin' with Shad, did ever you hear of this place, Shiloh?"

He shook his head. "It's no town, I guess. Jest a little church near Pittsburg Landing that got caught up in the midst of all the fightin'." Nancy was like his mother, he thought; one couldn't tempt her away from the sadness within her.

"I couldn't sleep after I read the papers Jenny brought me. I kept thinkin' of the two young boys—and Bill—and of John bein' in battles later on. I thought the night was goin' to go on ferever." She broke off suddenly and sat looking out across the quiet field, her hands folded in her lap. "What do you s'pose it was like, Jeth?"

He shook his head. "It must ha' seemed like the end of the world had come," he said soberly.

"Fer thousands it had, hadn't it?"

He nodded and felt ashamed that his anger over Shad's letter had made him forget the battle and the thousands of boys lying on the ground at a place called Shiloh. Ed Turner had said, "You can't expect to hear from the boys fer a while, Jeth. Think what a job it's goin' to be to clear the battleground." Jethro pushed the thoughts back in his mind; he didn't want to talk to Nancy about things like that.

He knew that it was time to be getting back to work, but when he started to get up Nancy stopped him with a quick gesture.

"Set a minute longer, Jeth. There's somethin' I feel bound to say to you."

He looked at her with surprise. "What's this thing that's on yore mind?" he asked, settling back comfortably against the tree trunk and looking up at small segments of sky that appeared here and there through the canopy of green leaves.

Nancy hesitated, and when she finally spoke, her words came slowly as if she were feeling her way with caution.

"You mustn't hold it aginst little Jenny that she keeps her letter to herself, Jeth. A letter is kind of a close thing; it's somebody's words that are writ only fer you. It's like you're bein' unfair to someone you love if you let his words be read by others when he writ 'em only fer you."

Jethro frowned and stared at the blue patches above him without comment.

"Sometime you'll know what I mean," Nancy continued. "Likely there's some little gal—maybe one not yet born—that will write to you some day, and every word she writes will be yores. You'll feel that you can't bring yoreself to share them words, because they won't belong to anyone but you."

Jethro shifted his position uneasily. He picked up a small stone and heaved it into the weeds in front of him.

"I doubt that," he muttered. "I don't care nothin' about any girl."

"When you was six, I guess you'd ha' doubted that soon you'd be managin' a team and plow by yoreself. I guess you'd ha' doubted that by the time you was ten you'd be workin' to put food in the mouths of yore brother's little 'uns—ain't that so, Jeth?"

"I reckon."

She placed her hand on his knee for a second. "I'd best let you git to yore work and go back to my own," she said. She called the children and got slowly to her feet.

"John used to want me to talk more to the folks around me. It was hard fer me to do it then; now, seems when I find someone to talk to, it's all I kin do to make myself go back to the stillness."

Jethro was exhausted that night. Jenny came out to the barnlot when she saw him dragging home with the tired team.

"Go eat yore supper, Jeth. I'll unhitch and water the horses fer you."

Jethro was not yet in any mood approaching perfect sweetness and light.

"Tendin' a team is man's work," he said grimly. "I'll do my own unhitchin' and waterin'."

"I've bin sharin' a man's work, don't fergit that." Jenny's dark eyes flashed with quick anger, but they softened as she looked at his thin body, sagging with fatigue.

"No use in bein' stubborn as a mule jest because it comes easy to you, Jeth." She started undoing the traces and tossed her head at him.

"Go on up to the house, young man. I got in early and made a nice puddin' fer yore supper. You're lucky to have a sister that is one of the best cooks in the county—don't ever think you're not."

Oh, she was in a gay mood, that Jenny. The words in Shad's letter that no one else had a right to read must have been extra fine!

Jethro shrugged ungraciously and went up to wash himself at the big iron kettle beside the kitchen well. The cool water felt good; he splashed it behind his ears and on his face and neck. He remembered once when Tom and Eb were washing at the kettle, and they had splashed him with cold water when he came to watch them. He had cried then, being pretty young, and the big fellows had called him a baby. He remembered that he'd felt strange and lonesome when they teased him, but suddenly Bill was there, and Bill had said, "I don't know whether it's more babyish to cry or to tease a little feller."

Tom had tried to make it up to Jethro later. It may have been the gift of an apple or the right to sit in front of the saddle that evening when they rode off on some errand—Jethro couldn't quite remember—but whatever it was, Tom had been extra kind to him. He hoped they'd get a letter soon from somewhere down in Tennessee.

Jethro was not able to read the paper after supper that night. He was tired to the bone, and he climbed off to his bed in the loft as soon as he finished the pudding Jenny had made for him. He was sound asleep before the spring night was quite dark, but excessive fatigue, like excitement, was a forerunner of the nightmares that had plagued him for the past year.

It was not quite midnight when some frightening dream made him cry out, and now that Bill was no longer there to comfort him, it was Jenny who ran from her room to sit on his bed and speak comfortingly.

"Maybe you drove yoreself too hard today, Jeth. I guess you've made yoreself over-tired."

"I'm all right," he said after a minute. "You don't hev to stay here; I'm awake now."

"You air mad at me, ain't you, Jeth?"

"I'm not mad at anybody. I'm jest sleepy," he answered shortly.

"The reason I didn't pass my letter around, Jeth— well, you know how Pa is—he thinks I'm so young and hadn't ought to think about gittin' married—and Shad said some things—"

"I don't care about yore letter. I don't want to read it."

"But you kin, Jeth; I'll let you read it. Nobody else, jest you."

"No," he said, turning his head away from her.

She was silent, and he suffered during the silence, knowing that he had hurt her. Finally he reached out and touched her hand.

"I don't want to read words that was writ jest fer you, Jenny. That ain't right. Me and Nancy—Nancy and I—talked about it some this afternoon."

Jenny bent and kissed his forehead; he did not mind, really, but he was a little embarrassed.

"You kin go back to bed; I ain't worried about my dream now."

As Jenny was leaving she stopped for a moment at the open door, where a ladder led down to the dooryard.

"Do you hear horses, Jeth?" she asked in a whisper.

He sat up in bed listening. The sound was faint at first, but after a short time they could hear plainly the beat of hoofs on the hard-packed road.

It had not been unusual in other days, when the country was full of young men, to hear riders late at night, but there were few young men left in the community now; moreover, at this season most horses were being used in the fields, and at this hour of the night were quietly grazing or resting after the long day's work in the fields.

"It's two or three horses gallopin' together," Jethro said in a low voice. He shivered a little. There was something ominous in the hoofbeats. He heard his parents stirring downstairs; Jenny's hand clutched his, and he could feel it trembling.

At about a quarter of a mile from the house, the galloping hoofbeats quieted suddenly; shortly afterward, the two watchers at the cabin could see the dim outline of three horses carrying men who seemed to be crouching close to the horses' necks. There was a fearful stillness about their approach until they were within a few yards of the gate; then there was a sudden wild shout, and a horse reared as if in fright at the sound. Jethro heard someone shout his father's name and Bill's and the word Copperheads.

Matt fumbled his way to the front door. "Show yore faces," he called. "Come up and give me a chance to talk."

There was only raucous, drunken laughter at his words. A bundle of something was thrown at the gate, and then the riders galloped on.

Jethro scrambled down the ladder and ran out into the yard. At the gate there was a bundle of switches tied together with a cord, the symbol adopted by local ruffians as a warning of punishment to follow. He tore off the paper that was attached to the cord and carried it inside to the table, where Ellen had lighted a lamp. On the paper in large printed letters was the message: "Theres trubel fer fokes that stands up fer there reb lovin sons."

Matt sat down heavily in the chair Jenny brought for him. "This war is a beast with long claws," he said in a choked voice.

They were all silent for a minute; then Ellen went to the door, lifted the gun that was held on hooks above the casing, and laid it carefully on the floor beside the bed.

During the next three weeks someone lay out in the yard with a gun at his hand every night. Israel Thomas came, and his son-in-law, Henry Giles; Ed Turner and his boys took turns; Sigurd Nelson from out toward Old Grandville and Irv Chandler from Hidalgo volunteered a night each week. The greater part of the community was enraged that a sick man should be thus tormented, and they hoped the night prowlers would soon show up to get a taste of what Matt Creighton's neighbors thought of them.

That was the feeling of the greater part of the community, but not all of it. Some men turned their backs when Matt's troubles were talked about in their presence. One man said to Israel Thomas, "How do I know it wasn't Bill Creighton's bullet that shattered my boy's leg at Pea Ridge?"

"It wasn't Matt's bullet," Israel Thomas retorted, "nor was it young Tom's or Eb's or John's."

"No, but like they air a-sayin' down in Newton, Matt's young 'un made it plain that the fam'ly still sticks up fer Bill."

Nancy, frightened at being alone, came up with the children to sleep in Jenny's room each night. The two girls were up at dawn each morning to prepare a hot breakfast for the men who had lain out in the yard on guard during the night.

When nothing happened during the rest of the month, the men decided that the switches had been an empty threat. It was the peak of the planting season, and the nights spent on the hard ground took their toll of men whose endurance was needed for the hard daily work in the fields. They cautioned Jethro to tie the dog up near the cabin each night so that he might warn the family of anyone approaching, and

Ed Turner brought up an old dinner bell, which he attached to a post close to the kitchen door.

"If there's any trouble, you ring this, Jeth. Some of us is bound to hear it, and we'll come," Ed promised.

None of the Creightons slept well at night for a while, until exhaustion overcame their anxieties. Jenny's face was drained of some of its rich color these days, and Jethro's had a grayish cast under his bright hair. The dark was a fearful thing, but as the hours of the night wore on, sleep came to them anyway. They would just have to meet the attack if it came; they had no strength to lie and worry about it.

As the days passed, the family's fears began to be allayed. Not even the disappearance of the big shepherd dog gave them too much concern. Nancy's oldest boy, Billy, told Jeth that he had seen a man patting Shep, and when the man whistled Shep went running after him. It was not unusual for someone passing through the neighborhood to coax away a valuable-looking dog. Jethro was annoyed at Shep's gullibility, but not particularly anxious.

"He'll be back, Billy, with his tail between his legs," Jethro told the little boy. "He'll git homesick and find some way to git back to us—you'll see."

But Shep didn't come back, and a few nights after his disappearance Jethro was awakened by the smell of smoke and the crackle of burning hay and wood. When he ran to the door he saw the barn enveloped in flames that leaped far into the sky; hay, grain, wagon, harnesses, and plows were feeding them, and they were hungry. There was one condition that must have been a matter of chagrin for the arsonists—all the farm animals were turned out to pasture during the summer nights and so escaped a fiery death.

Ellen, the two young women, and Jethro stood in the yard and watched silently. Matt wept as he leaned against the door-casing.

Israel Thomas saw the flames from his home a mile away, and Ed Turner had been awakened by the smell of smoke only minutes before he heard the ringing of the dinner bell. They and others came shortly, and they stayed throughout the night to see that the burning brands were not blown onto the roof of the cabin.

When the barn was burned to a pile of glowing coals, the men asked Jethro to draw water from the stock well to throw around the edges of the coals. He was conscious of a foul odor when he emptied the first bucketful into the kettle beside the well.

It was coal oil. That was a kind of punishment favored by mobs and self-appointed judges—coal oil in the culprit's well. It could cause him any amount of labor and anguish; it took little time or intelligence or skill, and it released most effectively the malice and spite of those who took punishment into their own hands.

Chapter 7

MEN from all over the county came to Matt Creighton's aid that spring. From as far away as Newton, Ross Milton and Sam Gardiner were able to collect enough for a set of double harness and a wagon; one man brought over a plow; others brought in loads of grain and hay for summer feeding. They cleaned his well, and more than a dozen offered a day's work in the fields whenever they had time to spare it. Immediate neighbors gave Matt their promise of raising a new barn as soon as the pressure of summer work had eased a little, and a dozen men from other communities volunteered their services in the project.

The great mound of ashes in the barnlot was soon beaten into a hard-packed mass by driving rain and the heat of spring and early summer. Jethro became used to the sight of it after a while, but he could not become used to the fear that lived with him every night during the early weeks of that summer. One of Ed Turner's boys brought over a dog to take the place of the shepherd that was never found. It was a huge dog, as fierce looking as a wolf, but soon devoted to Jethro after young Sam Turner had taught the boy how to become the dog's master. It brought some comfort to every member of the family to know that the big animal lay stretched at the foot of Jethro's bed, his sharp ears alert to every sound outside the cabin. But from Matt down to John's youngest boy there was a nagging fear that even the presence of the dog did not dispel altogether, an anxiety that lurked in the backs of their minds by day and came out boldly in the night.

More and more stories of Shiloh came through to the county as Illinois boys who had been wounded in the battle began pouring into Cairo, Illinois, during the months of May and June. George Lawrence from over near Grandville heard that his youngest son had arrived in the river town, and he made the long trip by wagon to bring the wounded boy back home. It was Dan Lawrence who brought news of Tom Creighton.

Israel Thomas and his son-in-law had volunteered a day's work in Matt's fields the day George Lawrence brought his boy over to the farm. They stopped their horses at the end of the furrow and went out to the road to talk to the two in the wagon; later they called to Jethro asking him to tell Ellen that they would not be up to dinner that day; they would work straight through the noon hour and go home a little early.

Dan Lawrence was not yet twenty; he was still weak from his wounds and loss of blood, still under the cloud of a horror that only subsequent horrors could make him forget. He walked slowly with his father's help up the path to the cabin where Matt Creighton stood at the door, and when Dan extended his hand in greeting, his eyes had a tired, haunted look. His father spoke for him.

"We're bringin' you hard news, Matt. It's yore boy Tom. I'd ruther be whipped than be the bearer of sich news, but we knowed we had to do it. I brung Danny over to tell you how it was. He was with yore boy that day."

Dan Lawrence told the story quietly. His voice wasn't as firm as a soldier's voice should be, but he did his best to control it.

"Things had bin so fine fer quite a spell—I never seed a part of the country that looked purtier, with the peach trees in bloom and the air so soft and lazy. Us boys was feelin' good. There was lots of time fer swimmin' and settin' around and talkin' about what we'd do when oncet the Rebs was licked and we was home agin. Tom and me was together a lot them days, and we done a good deal of laughin' and jokin'—Tom's spirits was allus high. You wouldn't ha' believed in them first days of April that trouble was a-brewin' fer all of us—ever' one was feelin' good, and we was gettin' along so fine." The young soldier glanced up at the white faces watching him, and there was still in his eyes the look of wonder that life could have changed so suddenly and ruthlessly. He seemed to waver before the necessity of describing the day that followed the first five of that April.

"It started at breakfast time, all of a sudden—and terr'ble. I ain't never heered sich noise, or seed so many boys and men laid low. It was jest one awful roar of cannon and screams—that was the worst. Maybe I hadn't ought to say these things—" he looked timidly toward Ellen, who sat close to her husband, her great dark eyes staring and without expression.

Matt finally spoke. "We want to hear everything, Danny; go ahead."

"We'd got through the first day, and tow'rd evening Buell's reinforcements commenced to come in from across the Tennessee River, and it was a sight that give us courage and joy—fer a few minutes, anyway. Tom was standin' beside me when we seed the boats comin', and both of us took off our caps and waved and laughed like we was crazy. We was caked with mud and tired enough to drop, but we fergot everything when we seed Buell's boys comin' in to help us. I mind that Tom put his arm 'long side my shoulders, and he was sayin', 'Look at 'em come, Danny; bless ol' Buell, he's fin'ly made it.' Them was his last words. He—he didn't suffer; he never knowed what happened."

The news spread through the county very quickly. The week after Dan Lawrence's story had been heard in Newton, Ross Milton printed an open letter in his paper.

TO THE PATRIOTS WHO DEFILED THE WELL AND BURNED THE BARN ON MATTHEW CREIGHTON'S FARM SOMETIME DURING THE NIGHT OF MAY 10TH, 1862:

Gentlemen:
In the event that you feel Matt Creighton has not been sufficiently punished by the destruction of his property, be advised that he suffers not only that loss through your efforts, but the loss of his nineteen-year-old son, who died in the battle of Pittsburg Landing on April 6th.

Has justice been done, Gentlemen? Has an ailing man who commands the respect of those in this county who recognize integrity—has this man suffered enough to satisfy your patriotic zeal?

May I remind you that Tom Creighton died for the Union cause, that he died in battle, where a man fights his opponent face to face rather than striking and scuttling off into the darkness?

And just in passing, Gentlemen, what have you done lately for the Union cause?

Of course you have burned a man's property—barn, farm implements, hay, and grain; you have polluted his well with coal oil and terrified his family. Furthermore, you have done it quietly, under cover of darkness, never once asking to be recognized in order to receive the plaudits of the country at large. But, has any one of you faced a Confederate bullet? Well, Matt Creighton's boy has.

Jenny cut the letter from their copy of Ross Milton's newspaper and placed it inside the cover of the family Bible. Then she turned to the pages where the family names were written in a long column with places to the right for dates of birth, marriage, and death. She dipped a pen in ink and carried it and the Bible to her father.

Matt shook his head. "You write a better hand than I do, Jenny; you set down the date and place for me. I've done it so often—too many times." He would not watch Jenny write, but motioned to Ellen to help him walk outside under the silver poplars in the dooryard.

Jethro sat at his sister's side and studied the page to which she had turned. His own name was at the bottom of the long list—Jethro Hallam Creighton, born January 13th, 1852.

"That was the name of the old doctor that the folks set such store by," Jenny explained. "Dr. Jethro Hallam. I remember him just a little. He used to hold me on his lap, and once he give me candy because I didn't cry when he had to swab my throat."

Jethro looked at her respectfully. She knew people and times unknown to him. He could not agree with his father that Jenny was so very young.

Directly above his name were three lines that his father had filled out just ten years ago that summer.

MATTHEW COLVIN CREIGHTON, BORN
SEPTEMBER 7TH, 1850. DIED JULY 1ST, 1852.
JAMES ALEXANDER CREIGHTON, BORN MAY
3RD, 1849. DIED JULY 4TH, 1852.
NATHAN HALE CREIGHTON, BORN FEBRUARY
12TH, 1848. DIED JULY 3RD, 1852.

The tragedy of that summer had never impressed Jethro so deeply as it did that afternoon when the dates stared up at him with terrible significance.

"Do you remember them, Jenny?" he asked soberly.

"Oh, yes. They're growin' more and more dim in my mind, though. I can remember that Ma set me to rockin' little Matt's cradle once, and I got so carried away with my singin' to him that I rocked the cradle too hard and the little round baby rolled right out onto the floor. That stands out in my mind—I was so fearful that I'd hurt him." Jenny smiled a little. "We was always wantin' to hold the youngest one; lots of times Mary and me and even Nate would fuss over who was to hold you next. Ma would say, 'Wait till he starts cryin'; then we'll see who wants him,' and sure enough, once the cryin' started, we was ready to hand you over."

It seemed very far away and unreal to Jethro. "Sometimes I forget that they was older than I am. I always think of them as the little boys."

"I reckon that's the way it'll always seem—they'll never be old."

"It seems strange, don't it, Jenny, that the sickness struck the three of them and passed over the rest of us?"

She nodded. "It's a thing no one can explain. I remember that Israel Thomas took Mary and Tom home with him—Eb wasn't yet with us—and Bill took you and me over to Ed Turner's. He carried you in his arms and led me by the hand, almost like he was our pa, though he wasn't much more than a boy then. Some of our folks made the rounds every day to see about us—they was so fearful that the disease might strike more of us. But we stayed well; it was a miracle."

Her name was next on the list—Jenny Elizabeth Creighton; then the name Mary Ellen Creighton, with the date of her death, January 12th, 1859, written far out in the righthand column. Above was the line Jenny must fill out: Thomas Ward Creighton, born May 10th, 1843. She made the notation, Died at Pittsburg Landing, April 6th, 1862, with great care and she wiped her eyes quickly lest the ink of the record be smudged.

The long list climbed on. In the years 1837 and 1838 John Robert and William Taylor were born, the two who had once been closest in affection—cut from the same bolt, Ellen had said. Above these were three other names that belonged to complete strangers as far as Jethro was concerned. The twin girls, Lydia and Lucinda, long since married and moved to Ohio, were born in 1834. The name at the top of the list was Benjamin Hardin Creighton, born in 1832. After his name Matt had written: Left for Californy in 1849.

"I wonder if he ever found any gold," Jethro mused.

Jenny shook her head, and he noticed that her face looked very tired. To cheer her, he pointed to the space for a marriage date opposite her name.

"Some day we'll be writin' in this space: Married to Shadrach Yale—and then your weddin' date."

The smiles and blushes that usually came at the mention of Shadrach were missing that day; Jenny's dark eyes were very large and grave.

"I'm so scared, Jeth. Seems I hadn't known what war was till Danny Lawrence come bringin' us this awful word of Tom." She closed the Bible and crossed her forearms on its faded cover. "I used to dream about the nice home Shad and me would have and how I'd keep it bright and pretty, how I'd wait of an evenin' to see him comin' down the road toward home. Nowadays I don't make any plans; I just don't dare to have any dreams for fear someday a soldier will come home and tell us that he was standin' beside Shad, the way Danny was standin' beside Tom—"

She got up abruptly and put the Bible back on the shelf among the books Shadrach had left. Together she and Jethro walked silently out to the barnlot and got their team ready to go back to the fields.

They needed recreation and laughter as they needed food. In other years the little house had buzzed with the teasing and squabbling and hilarity of a crowd of young people. There had been dances and cornhuskings and candymakings throughout the neighborhood; there had been afternoons of horseshoe pitching and evenings of charades. Shadrach had organized a singing school for winter nights, and sometimes there was a spelldown at the school followed by a box supper, which was partly a fundraising project and partly an opportunity for romantic developments. Jethro had not participated in these activities, but he had watched the fun from the sidelines, and that had been enough; some of the laughter and gaiety had overflowed to touch him, and he had felt himself a part of it.

Now the cabin had the look of a lonely old man

brooding in the summer sunlight. Beyond the chatter of Nancy's little boys, there was no lightness within the cabin or anywhere nearby. In New York, of course, the papers stated that society had never been so gay; that the sale of jewels and fine fabrics and sundry baubles of high fashion had never been so great. People were going to the opera, to balls, to glittering dinners in the great hotels, in spite of casualty lists and the fact that the war showed no signs of ending.

In Jasper County, however, laughter was a scarce luxury that summer, but as the weeks of 1862 marched on toward fall, an incident occurred that appealed to the rough humor of the times and to the satisfaction of many who saw justice finally finding a niche for itself. It was an incident that brought down a storm of ridicule upon Guy Wortman, was welcomed by those who had shuddered before the picture of mob violence spreading throughout the county as it had downstate, and was as effective in silencing Wortman as a prison term would have been.

The incident revolved about Sam Gardiner, the pudgy, round-faced proprietor of the general store in Newton. Gardiner had minced no words in his anger over what had happened at the Creighton farm that spring, and knowing what to expect from the Wortman-led element in the county, he stayed night after night in his darkened store waiting for an attack and his chance to answer it. He was a marksman of no mean ability; he was, moreover, stubbornly tenacious under his mild manner—two facts well-enough known around town to make the night prowlers wary for several weeks. The newspaper office was broken into and valuable material destroyed; Lafe Edwards' saloon was given similar treatment; but the general store was untouched.

Finally Sam Gardiner grew tired of waiting and taunted his foes by taking on a role of smugness and boasting of his immunity to Wortman's vengeance. After a few days he took pains to let the community at large know that his store was to be closed for a week while he went to St. Louis on business. At Olney he waved to some acquaintances from Newton as he boarded the train; then, getting off at the first stop, he was brought back to Newton during the night by an accomplice. In the darkness he climbed to the loft of his store, where he stayed for three days, living on cold provisions from his stock and biding his time.

On the third night the ruffians struck. A back window was pried open, and the vandalism was proceeding in full force when a blast of buckshot sent three men leaping into the darkness and caught Guy Wortman, as Gardiner had intended it to do, directly in the hindquarters.

The rest was comic opera. A doctor was summoned to the scene, and a crowd of men soon gathered in the store where the round little merchant, in his nightshirt, held a lamp aloft to light the doctor's work, and clucked in gentle sympathy while the buckshot was dug from the backsides of a moaning Wortman.

Men all over the county roared at the story Ross Milton embellished with cutting sarcasm and published in his weekly paper, a story that caused Wortman to be demoted, even by his own lieutenants, from the role of a swaggering desperado to that of an inept and ridiculous figure, whining in his misery. Sam Gardiner's blast of buckshot brought a number of people to their senses and gave to a number of others the blessed gift of a night's sleep free of anxiety and terror.

While the county paper carried details of Guy Wortman's humiliation, the city papers carried a war story that had its own overtones of the ridiculous. General Halleck had shuffled the generals at Pittsburg Landing after the battle there, assigning Grant to an ineffectual position as assistant commander and taking command of the field himself. Then there had begun a snaillike approach of the Union Army toward Corinth, where General Beauregard had withdrawn with the Confederate Army—day after day of digging entrenchments, marching a little distance, stopping to dig more entrenchments. Grant had been criticized for not entrenching at Pittsburg Landing; Halleck, it seemed, was determined to entrench himself all the way from Pittsburg Landing to Cornith.

Then came the entry into Corinth. Northern newspapers, never very warm toward Halleck, wrote with a note of glee in their bitterness of the hoax by which Beauregard had managed to evacuate his sick and enfeebled army, thereby leaving for Halleck a deserted railroad town. General Halleck had confidently expected to bag an enemy, which he had reported to the War Department as being nearly 200,000 strong. Beauregard had withdrawn from Corinth leaving campfires burning, dummy guns with dummy cannoneers behind them, and a few drummer boys to play in the deserted streets, as if Confederate soldiers by the hundred thousands were still there to listen. Freight cars rattled through Corinth all during the night, covering the sound of withdrawal; and shrill rebel yells from the remainder of the army greeted the arrival of each train, suggesting that reinforcements were arriving by the hour.

Halleck occupied Corinth the next day, it was true, but there was an empty ring to his boast that this was a "victory as brilliant and important as any recorded in history." The papers suggested that perhaps it was Beauregard who, by managing to save the remnants of his army, had won something approaching a victory.

Jethro sat on the edge of the kitchen porch, fondling the dog as it nuzzled against his knee and looking out at the fields, where twilight was rapidly draining the green and gold from corn and wheat fields that stretched out below and beyond Walnut Hill. His eyes were wide and troubled with his thoughts. He had a high respect for education, for authority of men in high places, and yet the stories in the newspapers made him wonder. McClellan, the most promising young officer in his class at West Point, was now the general who either didn't move at all or moved ineffectually; Halleck, the author of a book on military science, was now the author of boasts that somehow branded him as a little man, even to a country boy who was hungry for a hero. There were stories of generals jealously eyeing one another, caring more for personal prestige than for defeating the Confederates; there were Pope and Sheridan, who blustered; there was Grant and the persistent stories of his heavy drinking. Nowhere in the North was there a general who looked and acted the part as did the Confederates' Lee and Jackson.

"What's the matter, Cap?" Jethro said aloud, bending down to look into the dog's deep eyes. "Ain't we in the right? And how does it happen, if we're in the right, that the Lord lets Jeff Davis get men like Lee and Jackson and gives us ones like McClellan and Halleck?"

That, in essence, was what men in high places were wondering that late summer; it was what the President himself was wondering, and the thousands of soldiers who were coming nearer, day by day, to Antietam, to Fredericksburg, and to Chancellorsville.

Chapter 8

THE autumn of '62 was grim. Looking back to the spring and early summer, Jethro realized that, although the early months had meant anxiety and fear for himself and his family, the cause of the Union had been going well in the West. He counted the Federal victories beginning with Fort Henry and Fort Donelson, always to be associated in his memory with that last firelit evening he had spent with Shadrach—on to Pea Ridge, from which Mr. Roscoe's grandson had emerged unharmed—to the Mississippi, where grim old Admiral Farragut had done the impossible and had taken over New Orleans, and where General Pope, blusterer though he might be, was hailed as a hero after he had taken New Madrid and the powerful Confederate fort at Island No. 10.

Jethro studied the map of the Mississippi carefully. Only a strip of the river between Baton Rouge and Vicksburg was then under Confederate control.

"We're doin' better than Shad allowed we would," he told Jenny. He measured the short strip on the map with his fingers. "Look, it's just a little piece of river; once we take that, it's like Shad told me—the Confederacy will be cut in two."

It was a very short strip as measured by his fingers, but a shadow swept across his eyes as he recalled Shadrach's words, "Think how hard the fighting was at this little dot on the map called Donelson." He thought of another dot, which was only peach orchards and an old church, where Tom and thousands of others had died—a dot that seemed a hateful place to him. He would have to grow older and learn from history that the battle had been one of great importance for the Union, that the Confederate attempt to regain western Tennessee had failed and was therefore a bitter blow to the government of Jefferson Davis. But in 1862, Jethro hated to think of Shiloh, not only because of Tom, but because it seemed to him to have been an empty victory.

The triumphs along the Mississippi had made good news, and hopes throughout the North were at a high peak when chilling word came up from Tennessee. There two Confederate generals, Bragg and Smith, had driven the Federals out of the Cumberland Gap and were moving north to Kentucky, where they would surely reclaim that state if Don Carlos Buell couldn't stop them. Young Tom had helped to clinch Kentucky to the side of the Union at Donelson; now Jethro read with a heavy heart that General Bragg was boasting of his intention to set up a Confederate governor of Kentucky.

Equally chilling was the news from the East. General Pope, hero of Island No. 10, was no longer a hero in Virginia. At the end of August, just thirteen months after the day when congressmen and their ladies had driven out to Bull Run for a day of picnicking and battle-viewing, a second disaster for the Federals took place on the same spot. The Confederate generals were Lee and Stonewall Jackson, together with James Longstreet, who brought up reinforcements that saved the day for the Confederates. A good part of McClellan's army, as well as Pope's, the papers admitted, was disorganized and hopeless.

Thus the high hopes that had given comfort to the

North during the spring were almost crushed by early fall. Faith in the leaders was at its lowest ebb, criticism of the President poured in from all sides, armies were demoralized, and desertion began, first in a slow trickling, then in a flood, as the months dragged on. Jethro read the news in dismay, and for the rest of the war there was always a fear within him that disappointment and disaster inevitably followed hope.

But work on the farm had to go on although armies faltered and leaders fell in disgrace. Late in September, men from the nearby communities and from even as far away as Newton came to build a new barn, so that Matt Creighton's stock might have shelter before the winter snows set in. There were twenty or more of them with teams and loads of logs, with saws and axes, and a barrel of cider to give their work a spark of holiday spirit. Ross Milton came, and although he was too crippled to work, the men were pleased to have him with them, and Jethro was delighted.

When he went out to greet the editor, Jethro noticed the young man who had cared for his team that day in Newton, now sitting on a high load of logs behind Ross Milton's buggy. Milton jerked his thumb toward the wagon as he climbed slowly down from his seat.

"Charley is bringing that load of logs from a friend of yours," he told Jethro quietly.

"I can't think of anybody down your way that is a special friend of mine," Jethro said, puzzled.

"Dave Burdow," the editor answered. "I'd asked him to come with us today. He wouldn't, but he came to town yesterday and asked me to have someone bring up this load of logs he'd cut. He said, 'Tell the young one Dave Burdow is sending them to him.'"

Jethro nodded. "I allow to get thanks—" he paused and flushed as he looked up at the editor. "I want to send thanks to him—one way or the other."

"I've done it for you," Milton answered, smiling briefly at the evidence that his book had been read. "Dave isn't used to thanks; they make him restless. But he's listened, and more than that, he's shaken several hands that have been extended to him since the two of you rode together through that stretch of woods road last March."

"I'm proud to hear it," Jethro said soberly.

"I thought you might be." Milton turned toward the porch, where Matt waited to speak to him, and Jethro went back to show Charley where to place his wagon and Burdow's gift.

By noon Ellen, with the help of Nancy and Jenny, had spread a long table out under the silver poplars in the dooryard, and here the men ate roasted meats and potatoes, vegetables preserved from the summer garden, baked beans, and corn bread spread thickly with freshly churned butter. They had autumn peaches picked from the trees and sliced in golden cream, mounds of wild honey, and apples that Nancy's little boys had polished until they gleamed rosily against the white cloth. The season of plenty in southern Illinois had not been touched by the war.

There might have been no war at all for an hour or so, as the men ate and joked in the mellow sunlight of the dooryard. But during the afternoon, as he carried water and ran a dozen different errands, Jethro heard them talk of a battle in the East. It was at a place he had not quite known how to pronounce when he had read of it in the papers. Antietam.

"Well, McClellan moved," Israel Thomas was saying, "you hev to say that fer him. He finally moved. Ol' Abe give him another chancet; maybe now he'll git down to fightin', if that ain't askin' too much of sech a fine-haired general."

Ed Turner's face was full of disgust as he strained to lift a log into place.

"Him git down to fightin'—don't ever think of it. He wants to strut around and brag and look han'some, but he don't want to fight—not him. I reckon Ol' Abe was right; the Army of the Potomac is Mr. McClellan's bodyguard."

"Well, he druv Bobby Lee out of Maryland t'other day," another man remarked. "That much is to his credit."

"And if Bobby Lee had druv McClellan out, he'd afollered up and apestered the army that was in retreat. But not McClellan. No, he wastes thousands of boys; then he sets back and rests, waitin' fer them that's left livin' to cheer him big." Ed Turner wiped the sweat from his eyes with an angry gesture. "I got no use fer McClellan. I don't know what Ol' Abe means—tuckerin' to him like he was some little sawed-off king."

Then Tom Marin from Rose Hill spoke up. "If you ask my opinion of McClellan, I'll tell you I don't think he *wants* to win. I don't think he's *ever* really goin' to move in on the Rebs, because their way of thinkin' is his way of thinkin'."

"Oh, I reckon he ain't *that* low. Ol' Abe must not be quite that pore in pickin' his head men," Israel Thomas objected.

"Maybe Ol' Abe ain't losin' *his* breath to lick the Rebs either—did ye ever think of that? Why is it he ain't freed the slaves? Is he afeared of hurtin' the feelin's of some of his woman's kinfolk down in Kaintuck? Why does he put up with this no-account that's runnin' the Army of the Potomac? Does he *like* seein' Bobby Lee run over us? I got a lot of questions about Ol' Abe that I'd like an answer to."

"Yore doubts ain't goin' to make me down on Ol' Abe, Tom," Israel Thomas answered angrily. "Things is tough right now, but this war is a big thing. It's middlin' easy fer us farmers and the big editors and the abolitionist preachers to run the job of bein' president. Ol' Abe is doin' all he *kin* do, I say, and I'm fer him—all the way."

One of the men took a drink from the water jug Jethro had brought up to the workers, and handing it back, he rumpled the boy's hair with rough affection.

"Be glad you're a boy, young feller, and don't hev to pester yoreself with all these troubles that men be sufferin' through these days," he said genially.

Jethro had picked up a mannerism from his mother. He closed his eyes briefly, as if to hide from the world the exasperation with which the man's words struck him. He knew he must keep quiet; these men were kind, generous men, and anyway, a boy had no right to contradict a man's opinion. If they wished to think of him as an ignorant child, he must not try to change their idea of him, but it was a bitter dose to swallow.

A few days after the barn-raising a letter came from Shadrach Yale in which he too discussed General McClellan, from the viewpoint of a young soldier who had just known his first experience under fire. Antietam had been the baptismal battle for the young schoolteacher, and the letter to Jenny reflected the agony of a man new to the scenes of death and suffering.

This time Jenny read the letter in its entirety to the family, and then she quietly passed it to her father and to Jethro for rereading. The words of love that interspersed those of mental anguish were not ones that a silly girl blushed over and hoarded to herself. There was a new dignity about Jenny after that letter from Antietam.

Of General McClellan, Shadrach wrote:

> *I have never known men of my age— and many much older—who have so completely worshipped another man. They may be hungry, wounded, heartsick at the death of comrades, but they forget everything when they see him, and they break into cheers as if this hero had brought them nothing but pure joy. They accept suffering of any kind as something through which they can show their devotion to this leader.*
>
> *You have probably read of the disorganization and discouragement of this army after General Pope's defeat at Bull Run. It took only the sight of this small, handsome man, McClellan, dashing up and down the lines on horseback to restore confidence and courage. He shouted, waved his cap, encouraged their cheers, and fired his men with the kind of spirit that they showed here at Antietam.*
>
> *The men resent those of us who have not known him long, the ones who are silent when they cheer. I believe that a word against him might be as dangerous to the one who spoke it as a Rebel bullet would be. They will not believe that he has ever been anything but right; they revile the President when rumors of his impatience with their general get around.*

I tell you frankly that the contagion of their devotion has not yet gripped me. I do not dislike him; I believe that he is personally brave and devoted to the cause for which his men are fighting. But he is afraid of something—of sending the men who love him to their death—of making an error that will reflect upon the image of himself which he knows to exist in the minds of his men. He does not have the cold approach to killing, the singleness of purpose, the brutal tenacity, that the winner of this war—if there ever is to be one—must have.

The autumn months approached the end of the year in gloom. Fields of green corn turned yellow, and the leaves, withered during the frosty nights, rattled as if in protest as Jethro drove his wagon down the rows and piled it high with full golden ears.

Antietam was over—a name for future history books, a battle at which men in later years, blessed with the advantage of hindsight, would wonder. Jethro, in his manhood, would learn of the incompetence, the blindness, and the ghastly waste of life that followed a lost opportunity; in the autumn of '62 he only knew that Antietam seemed much like Shiloh—a Federal victory in which one was hard put to find a step toward final triumph and peace.

The career of General McClellan was almost over, too; it would rise with another spurt later on, but that fall the papers blazed with the news that the President had relieved the general of his command, and the name that had outshone all others now plummeted into near-obscurity. Now another man dominated the headlines briefly—very briefly. The new name was that of Ambrose Burnside.

In December Jethro looked for another river and another town in Shadrach's atlas. The river was the Rappahannock in Virginia; the little town lying on the river was Fredericksburg.

The stories of the battle were ones that brought despair to the North. Fredericksburg had been undertaken with little probability of success, the papers claimed; nothing could have been expected under the shabby plans—if, indeed, they *were* plans—other than appalling slaughter. But Burnside was a stubborn man, determined perhaps to show action and confidence where McClellan had shown hesitancy and uncertainty. Wave after wave of men were sent up the slopes of a chain of hills from the tops of which the entrenched Confederates mowed the Federals down until the ground was piled high with blue-clad bodies. Rumor was that this general, far back from the line of battle, had insisted that still more divisions be sent up the deadly hills, but that he was finally dissuaded by officers of lower rank and keener perception.

Shadrach must have been at Fredericksburg; there could be little doubt of it. The family waited for days, during which Jethro's waking thoughts were filled with foreboding and his dreams with troubled anxiety. Jenny went about her work silently, and although there was work enough to tire the healthiest of young bodies, she took to going for long walks alone through the wintry fields, as Bill had once done. There was nothing one could say to comfort her.

Finally a letter came, word from Shadrach that he

was safe. He wrote:

> *It is unfortunate that congressmen and
> their ladies should have been deprived of
> this spectacle. There was drama here, I can
> tell them—thousands upon thousands of us
> crossing the Rappahannock with banners
> flying, drums rolling, and our instruments
> of death gleaming in the sunlight.
> They could have seen those thousands
> scrambling up the innocent-looking wooded
> hills and falling like toy soldiers brushed
> over by a child's hand; thousands of young
> men whose dreams and hopes were snuffed
> out in a second and who will be
> remembered only as simple soldiers who
> fell in a cruel, futile battle directed by men
> who can hardly be called less than
> murderers. I should not like to live with
> Ambrose Burnside's thoughts—though one
> wonders if his conscience is not protected
> by a thick covering of stubborn self-
> righteousness. Need I say that the men in
> the Army of the Potomac do not cheer
> General Burnside?*

In Tennessee there was a place called Stones River;
John was there, and in the early days of 1863 he
wrote to Nancy of what had happened in that battle.
He wrote of a commander named Rosecrans (Old
Rosy, the men called him) who had repulsed Van
Dorn (the Van Dorn of Pea Ridge, Jethro thought)
when the Confederates attempted to retake Corinth,
and had later replaced Don Carlos Buell when Buell,
too much the McClellan type of general, had been
relieved of his command. John wrote of bitter cold

and suffering that had finally ended with a victory of sorts when the Confederate General Bragg had left in full retreat, stopped short in his move toward Kentucky. Stones River was a victory, but there were thirteen thousand casualties, and John wrote wearily: *"The sufferin and scenes of deth was sech as to make a mans hart hate war."*

Fredericksburg and Stones River—the stories of these two battles filled the papers during the last days of 1862 and the early ones of 1863. Everyone was discouraged, and it looked as if the war might never be won; as if, indeed, the country that had been born in the travail of the Revolution and had been given direction during the days of 1787, when the Constitution came to life, might now be dissolved into two weak nations. Well, why not, soldiers were beginning to say. How much can men bear to keep together the nation their great-grandfathers had helped to create? They were losing faith—faith in their leaders and in the cause of union. In the late winter of 1862, the deserters began pouring back into Illinois. Thousands of young men had become disillusioned; this war was no "breakfas' spell."

Chapter 9

THE deserters came in droves. The Point Prospect campground south of Rose Hill was said to be swarming with soldiers who made forays on chicken coops, pigpens, and smokehouses where winter meat was hung. In the spring and summer, vegetable gardens, cornfields, and fruit orchards were robbed. No one dared to approach the camp. Even the U.S. agents from the cities upstate appeared to be in no hurry for a visit; it was known that the deserters carried their arms and that they were desperate. For a neighbor to have recognized a face among them might well have been sufficient reason for getting a bullet between the eyes; these men meant to take no chances with an informer.

The stories varied; some said there were a hundred men at Point Prospect; others put the number at nearer five hundred. In the early months of '63, the theft of food was their only crime against the community; by March, however, a killing took place.

There was a man known as Hig Phillips down in the southern part of the county, and the story came out that he had hired a substitute to go to war for him. That in itself was not uncommon; many others in the county had taken advantage of this method of dodging the draft, which in the spring of '63 included men from twenty up to the age of forty-five. Three hundred dollars was what it took; that was a lot of money, but once the substitute was found and the three hundred dollars paid, a man could sit back comfortably and yawn at the war news if he chose.

There were men who were forced to take

advantage of this system of substitute-hiring because of serious illness in the home or the dependency of motherless children. There was, however, no reason why Hig Phillips should have avoided the draft except that he was a lazy bachelor much favored by his mother, that he was fond of good food and a comfortable bed, and had been known to adhere to the opinion that fools could do the fighting while men of intelligence and property might take pleasure in the prospect of a long and easy life. He was not generally admired for these views, but that fact bothered him hardly at all.

Hardly at all, that is, until one moonless night a band of young men visited him—men who knew what gangrenous wounds were like, what marches through cold rain or blistering heat meant, while hunger gnawed at their stomachs or weakness from typhus or dysentery brought agony to every step; men who had seen the dead piled high on smoking battlefields and had come to believe that the soldier of two years had done his share, that the burden should now fall upon other shoulders.

Although there were many who held Hig Phillips in contempt, his murder was an act of lawlessness that terrorized the county. People realized that anything could be expected from a mob of undisciplined desperadoes. Nancy, who had thought of going back to her own place the following summer, now heeded Ellen's advice and closed her house completely, bringing her stock up to Matt's new barn and keeping her children in the comparative safety of their grandfather's home. Jenny was no longer allowed to drive alone to Hidalgo for the mail; no one ventured far away from home after nightfall, and as in the days of the Wortman trouble the year before, no one ever went to bed with the full confidence of security. The fury of the abolitionists and the Copperheads was now taken over by the deserters.

One night in February of '63, as the family sat around the open fire, a wagon clattered down the road from the north and stopped in front of the house. Opening the door, Jethro saw three young men jump down from the wagon and stride up to the porch.

"Is this the home of Matthew Creighton?" one of them asked. Jethro noticed the crispness of the voice—an upstate voice, he thought.

"Yes, sir, my father's right here. Will you come indoors?"

They came inside with a great clatter of heavy boots. Jenny stood, wide-eyed, beside her father's chair; Nancy and Ellen held the small boys tightly in their arms. Matt tried to rise.

"Stay seated, sir. We're here to ask you a few questions." The young man who spoke threw back his coat to show his uniform and insignia. "We are representatives of the Federal Registrars; we are charged with hunting down deserters from the United States Army."

"Will you take chairs, gentlemen?" Matt said evenly, but Jethro noticed the sudden paleness of his father's face.

"Thank you, no. We are here to inquire if this is the home of Ebenezer Carron, 17th Illinois Infantry, Army of Tennessee."

"It is. This has bin Eb's home since he was a lad of ten or so."

"Have you seen him lately?"

"Why, no. Him and my son Thomas left together for the Army in August of '61. My own boy was kilt at Pittsburg Landing; we ain't heered from Eb but once since then."

"You know the penalty for shielding a deserter from the United States Army?"

"I do. Air you tellin' me that Eb is a deserter?"

"His commanding officer has reason to believe that he is and that he has been making his way toward this part of the state—we assume toward his home."

Matt lifted a shaking hand and covered his eyes. Jenny glanced at him anxiously and then suddenly blazed out at the questioner.

"We haven't seen Eb. He's not here, and I'll thank you not to worry my father with more of this talk. If you want to look through this house—"

"We do, Miss—this house and all other buildings around here."

Jenny grasped the kerosene lamp with a firm hand. "Jeth, you come with me. We'll show these soldiers through the house; they can hunt outside for themselves."

Her anger made Jenny a very grand lady, Jethro thought. He had never seen her more beautiful than she was that night, with her cheeks flaming and her eyes large and black with mixed anger and fear.

The soldiers grinned a little among themselves and followed her and Jethro to the sleeping rooms in the loft, then down to the kitchen and pantry where Jenny took down the big key to the smokehouse and handed it to one of the men.

"We lock the smokehouse these nights. It's true there are deserters in these parts, and there's thievin' around everywhere. But we're not shieldin' anyone. Go look in the smokehouse for yourselves; go through the barn, the grainery, everywhere you think someone might be hidin'. After that I could say you'd best go down to the Point Prospect campground. The talk is that there are plenty of deserters there."

The Federal Registrars looked uncomfortable.

"Yes, we've heard," one of them muttered.

Jenny nodded. "It is easier to come to a house and upset a sick old man and scared womenfolk. Nobody in this neighborhood thinks it's healthy to go down to Point Prospect, but you sounded so brave just now—I thought you might want to do your duty down there."

The man who had done the questioning bowed mockingly before Jenny.

"We'll see to our duty, Miss, and if we find Ebenezer Carron on this place, we'll take him back with us—and maybe you, too." He turned toward Jethro. "Will you get a lantern, young man, and light us out back?"

Jethro took down the lantern that hung on the outside wall of the kitchen and started down the path toward the barn. The Federal Registrars followed, laughing with one another. One of them fell into step with Jethro after a time.

"Is that girl your sister?"

"Yes, sir."

"Well, she's quite a little beauty."

Jethro did not answer. His silence seemed to provoke the young man.

"I said that your sister is quite a little beauty, did you hear me?"

"She's spoke fer," Jethro answered shortly.

The young man shrugged and called out to the others. "I've just come upon some very interesting information: the beautiful little spitfire up at the ancestral mansion is 'spoke fer.'"

They laughed a great deal over that, and exaggerating the southern Illinois drawl and the backwoods diction, they made considerable sport over the boy's remark. Jethro felt his face burn with anger, but something new had been pointed up to him, something in the long process of learning to which he would be sensitive for the rest of his days. Until then he had not thought of his speech as being subject to ridicule.

The soldiers searched the place thoroughly and then started back to their wagon. One of them spoke sternly to Jethro on the way.

"If this man, Ebenezer Carron, turns up, you know what to do?"

"No, sir."

"Then you'd better listen. You get word to the Office of the Federal Registrars in Chicago right away, telling them where the man is or expects to be. You fail to report him, and you and your family will be up to your necks in trouble. Do you understand?"

Jethro nodded briefly. He was deeply antagonized by these men, but he knew they were simply carrying out a job assigned to them. Anyway, he was glad when the wagon carried them away—to the north. Evidently they were not going down to the deserters' camp at Point Prospect, not that night anyway.

There was an early spring that year. By the first of March the weather was warm, and the higher fields were dry enough for plowing. Jethro carried a rifle with him when he went down to John's place to work; Ellen fretted a great deal about it, but Matt insisted. Jethro had learned how to handle a gun properly, and it was always possible that he might bring down some kind of wild game for the table, or that he would have need to defend himself against a desperate man.

The field he plowed that day in early March was bordered on the east by dense woods, and Jethro became conscious that each time he approached the woods side of the field, the sharp, harsh call of a wild turkey would sound out with a strange kind of insistence—almost as if some stupid bird demanded that he stop and listen. Once when he halted his team and walked a little distance toward the woods, the calls came furiously, one after the other; then when he returned to his team and moved toward the west, they stopped until he had made the round of the field.

After several repetitions of this pattern, Jethro tethered his team and, taking up his rifle, walked into the woods. His heart beat fast as he walked, and his slim, brown hand clutching the rifle was wet with sweat. Ed Turner was giving him a day's help in the field across the road, but Jethro chose not to call him although he had a guilty feeling that he was taking a foolish and dangerous chance.

He walked slowly and carefully, pausing now and then to listen. The calls stopped for a while, and he was half convinced that they had actually come from a wild bird; he made no move for a few minutes, and they began again, softer now and more certainly coming from the throat of a man.

Jethro stood quite still. "Hello," he called finally. "What is it you want of me?"

There was no answer. Then the call came again, softly, insistently, from a clump of trees, one of which was a tremendous old oak—long since hollowed out, first by lightning and then by decay.

Jethro walked closer, his gun raised, and after a minute, the human voice which he had been half expecting to hear called out to him.

"Put yore gun down, Jeth; I ain't aimin' to hurt ye. I didn't dast take the chancet of Ed Turner hearin' me call to ye."

He thought joyfully of Bill at first. He shouldn't have; almost every night he heard his parents talking of Eb and of what uncertainties they would face if he were really a deserter and if he should suddenly appear. But Jethro had forgotten Eb for the moment; the possibility of Bill's return was always a hope far back in his mind.

"Who is it?" he asked again. "Come out and let me see your face."

Then a skeleton came out from among the trees. It was the skeleton of a Union soldier, though the uniform it wore was so ragged and filthy it was difficult to identify. The sunken cheeks were covered with a thin scattering of fuzz; the hair was lank and matted. It fell over the skeleton's forehead and down into its eyes. The boy stared at it without speaking.

"Jeth, you've growed past all believin'. I've bin watchin' you from fur off, and I couldn't git over it—how you've growed."

Then Jethro realized who it was. "Eb," he exclaimed in a voice hardly above a whisper. "It's Eb, ain't it?"

There was utter despair in the soldier's voice.

"Yes," he said, "I reckon it's Eb—what there's left of him."

For a few seconds Jethro forgot the Federal Registrars and the fact that not only the word which preceded Eb, but his method of announcing himself gave credence to the suspicion that he was a deserter. But for those first few seconds Jethro could only remember that this was Eb, a part of the family, the boy who had been close to Tom, the soldier who would have more vivid stories to tell of the war than ever a newspaper would be able to publish. He held out his hand.

"Eb, it's good—it's so good to see you. Pa and Ma will be—" he stopped suddenly. He noticed that Eb ignored his outstretched hand.

"Yore pa and ma will be scairt—that's what you mean, ain't it? Scairt fer themselves and ashamed of me." He paused for a second and then added defiantly, "I deserted, you know; I up and left Ol' Abe's Army of the United States."

Jethro could only stare at his cousin; he could find no words.

"Desertin' ain't a purty word to you, is it? Well, I done it—I don't jest know why. We'd had another skirmish and there was dead boys that we had to bury the next day—and we'd bin licked agin. All at oncet I knowed I couldn't stand it no longer, and I jest up and left. Oncet a man has left, he's done fer. I've bin a long time gittin' home, and now that I'm here, it ain't no comfort."

"Eb, couldn't you just come up to the house and see them for a few hours or so? Couldn't you have a good meal and get cleaned up and tell the folks all you know about Tom?"

"I cain't. I could git 'em into awful trouble. Besides, they would prob'ly jest as soon not set eyes on the likes of me agin."

"But, Eb, if you can't come up to the house, what *did* you come for?"

Eb's face showed quick anger. "I come because I couldn't help myself, that's why. *You* don't know what it's like—you that was allus the baby and the pet of the fam'ly. There be things that air too terr'ble to talk about—and you want to see the fields where you used to be happy, you want to smell the good air of old Illinois so much that you fergit—you go crazy fer an hour or so—and then you don't dare go back."

He shivered and leaned back against a tree trunk as if just talking had taken more strength than he had to spend.

"Have you been down to the Point Prospect

camp?" Jethro asked after a while.

"A couple days. It's worse than the war down there with fellers afraid and gittin' meaner as they git more afraid. I didn't come back to be with soldiers anyway. I'm sick of soldiers, livin' and dead; I'm sick of all of 'em." He threw himself down on a thick padding of dead leaves and motioned Jethro to do the same.

"I want ye to tell me about 'em, Jeth—Uncle Matt and Aunt Ellen, Jenny . . ."

"You knew Pa had a heart attack; he's not been himself since. Ma's tolerable, and Jenny's fine. We do the work of the farm together, Jenny and me."

"And John, Shad—where air they? They jined up, didn't they?"

"Yes, John's in Tennessee under a general named Rosecrans. And Shad's in the East with the Army of the Potomac. He was at Antietam Creek and Fredericksburg; you heard of them two battles, didn't you?"

"We hear precious little except what's happenin' in the part of the country we're in. I've heered of Ol' Abe kickin' out that fine McClellan; it's a pity he don't kick out a passel of 'em out in the West." Eb seemed absorbed in his angry thoughts for a while; then he looked up at Jethro again.

"And Bill, did ever you hear from him?"

"Not a word," Jethro replied in a voice that was hardly audible.

"I guess you took that hard. You was allus a pet of Bill's."

"All of us took it hard."

"Yore pa wrote Tom and me about it. Tom tried to pretend he didn't keer, but I know he did. He cried oncet—I wouldn't tell that 'cept now it's no matter."

"No," Jethro agreed dully, "now it's no matter."

Eb took a dry twig and broke it up into a dozen pieces, aimlessly.

"How did you git the word about Tom?" he asked finally.

"Dan Lawrence was home on sick leave. His pa brought him over; he told us all about it."

"I was at Pittsburg Landing too, but I didn't know about Tom—not fer two or three days. I wanted to write, but somehow I couldn't do it. Tom and me had bin in swimmin' the day before the Rebs su'prised us; we was both of us in good spirits then, laughin' and carryin' on like we done in the old days back home. Somehow all the spirit in me has bin gone ever since. I could stand things as long as I had Tom along with me."

He ran his hand across his eyes as if to shut out a picture or a memory. "Tell me about little Jenny; is she still in love with Shad Yale?"

"More than ever, I guess. She writes to him a lot; he sets great store by her letters."

"He ought to. A man needs a girl's nice letters when he's sufferin' with the homesick. I wisht I'd had a girl like Jenny to write to me, but there ain't many such as her, I reckon."

Jethro studied Eb's sunken cheeks and dull eyes.

"How do you manage to eat, Eb?"

"I don't do it reg'lar, that's shore. I live off the land—steal a little, shoot me a rabbit or squirrel and cook 'em over a low fire late at night. It ain't good eatin', but nothin's good these days like it used to be."

Jethro's insides twisted in sympathy. "Are you hungry now, Eb?"

"I'm allus hungry. Ye git used to it after a while."

"Nancy fixed me some grub to bring to the field with me; I'll go get it for you."

He ran to the fencerow where he had left two pieces of bread and the cuts from a particularly tender haunch of beef that Nancy had wrapped in a white cloth for him. Ordinarily he would have eaten the snack by midafternoon, but the wild-turkey calls had made him forget it. He returned to Eb minutes later with the food and a jug of water.

They sat together in the shadows, while Eb ate with an appetite that was like a hungry animal's.

"Eb, I've got to tell you," Jethro said quietly after a while. "The soldiers that call themselves the Federal Registrars was at the house lookin' for you last month."

Eb seemed to shrink within himself. He looked at his hands carefully, as if he really cared about inspecting them, and his mouth worked in a strange, convulsive grimace. He wouldn't look at Jethro when he finally spoke.

"I was an awful fool—at least you got a chancet in battle—maybe it's one in a hunderd, but it's a chancet. This way, I got none. There's no place on this earth fer me to go. Even the camps of deserters don't want fellers as weak and sick as I am; they let me know that quick at Point Prospect. I'll either freeze or starve—or be ketched. I'd give jest about anythin' if I could walk back to my old outfit and pitch into the fightin' agin. A soldier don't have to feel ashamed."

Jethro sat for a while trying to think of some way out of the situation; it appeared more hopeless the more he thought. He was frightened—for the despairing man in front of him, for himself, and his family. When he finally spoke, he tried hard to sound reassuring, but the pounding of his heart made his voice shake.

"Well, you stay here till we can think of somethin',

Eb. I'm goin' to get you some quilts and things from Nancy's place; I'll bring you what grub I can lay hands on—I can always get eggs and a chicken for you. I think you'd best eat all you can and rest for a spell; we'll think of what's to be done when once you get a little stronger."

Eb looked up then. "You all but fool me into believin' that somethin' *kin* be done, Jeth, but I know better. You ner no one else kin help me now—not even Ol' Abe hisself."

Ol' Abe. Mr. Lincoln. Mr. President.

"I ought to go back to work now, Eb."

"I guess so," Eb looked at him with a suggestion of a smile. "I cain't git used to it—you bein' big enough to handle a team alone. You seem almost a man these days, Jeth; even yore hair ain't quite as yaller and curly as it used to be."

Jethro turned away. "I'll bring you a quilt from Nancy's before I go in for the night," he said shortly.

He walked back to his waiting team; there was still time to plow a dozen furrows before sunset—and to think.

He had faced sorrow when Bill left and fear the night Guy Wortman tried to pull him down from the wagon; he had felt a terrible emptiness the day Shadrach and John went away and deep anger the night he watched the barn burn at the hands of the county ruffians. But in his eleven years he had never been faced with the responsibility of making a fearful decision like the one confronting him.

The authority of the law loomed big in his mind; he remembered, "You and your family will be in serious trouble." Loyalty to his brother Tom and the many thousands who had fought to the last ditch at Pittsburg Landing, at Antietam, Fredericksburg, and all the other places that were adding length to the long list—how could loyalty to these men be true if one were going to harbor and give comfort to a man who simply said, "I quit."

But, on the other hand, how did one feel at night if he awoke and remembered, "I'm the one that sent my cousin to his death." Eb was not a hero, certainly—not now, anyway. People scorned the likes of Eb; sure, so did Jethro, and yet—

"How do I know what *I'd* be like if I was sick and scared and hopeless; how does Ed Turner or Mr. Milton or *any* man know that ain't been there? We got to remember that Eb has been in battles for two years; maybe he's been a hero in them battles, and maybe to go on bein' a hero in a war that has no end in sight is too much to ask. . . . Sure, deep down in me, I want Eb to get out, to leave me free of feelin' that I'm doin' wrong to give him grub, or takin' the risk of keepin' it a secret that he's here. Yes, it would leave me free if he'd just move on—but no, it wouldn't—I ain't goin' to be free when he moves on; I can't set down to a table and forget that someone sick as Eb looks to be is livin' off the land, that he's livin' scared like a wild animal that's bein' hunted.

"But what's it goin' to be like if more and more soldiers quit and go into the woods and leave the fightin' to them that won't quit? What do you say to yourself when you remember that you fed and helped someone like Eb and maybe you get a letter from the East that Shad is killed and you see Jenny grievin', or that John is killed and Nancy and her little boys is left all alone—how do you feel when things like that come up?

"Of course, right now I could say to Pa 'I leave it up to you'—and then what could he do? Why, he'd be caught in the same trap I'm in now; I'd wriggle out of it and leave the decidin' to a sick old man; I'd put him in the spot where any way he decided would be bad—hurtful to a man's conscience. No, there ain't an answer that's any plainer to an old man than it is to me. And what was it that man said the day of the barn-raisin'? 'It's good that you're a boy and don't have to worry yourself about this war.' Why yes, no doubt about it, eleven-year-old boys ain't got a thing to worry about; this year of 1863 is a fine, carefree time for eleven-year-old boys. . . ."

Jenny noticed his preoccupation at supper that night. She waited until the others were out of the kitchen, and she and Jethro were left alone.

"What is it that's on your mind, Jeth?"

"Nothin'. Just tired." He threw himself down in front of the fireplace and closed his eyes. He knew it would be hard to deceive his sister; there was a determination about Jenny.

"You'd better tell me, Jeth. I'll find out, you know."

"You don't give me any worry; there's nothin' to find out."

"Jeth, have you had some news about Shad or John?"

"No, how could I? You know what mail has come."

"You might ha' talked to someone."

"Well, I ain't. Not to anyone that knows a word about Shad or John."

She worked at her dishpan for a while in silence; then she walked over and poked him a little with the toe of her shoe.

"There's somethin', Jeth. Nancy noticed it too. Now I want to know—is it somethin' about Eb? Is he here with the deserters?"

He turned his head away from her; he couldn't remember when he had lied to Jenny, and he wasn't sure that he could do it well.

"Jenny, you vex me when I'm not feelin' so well. Can't I have an upset stummick without you firin' a passel of questions at me?"

She stood looking down at him thoughtfully for a while, and then an idea stemming from experience with older brothers suddenly struck her. She dropped down beside him and whispered her suspicion gleefully in his ear.

"Jeth Creighton, have you been smokin' on the sly? Is *that* what's givin' you an upset stummick?"

He kept his eyes closed and did not answer, knowing his silence would confirm her guess. Jenny was triumphant.

"That's it! I know without your sayin' it," she crowed. "You look white, the way Tom and Eb did once when they tried it."

It was very simple to lie without words; he merely opened his eyes and grinned sheepishly at her.

"I'm su'prised you would be that silly, Jeth. With so much spring work to do, you don't have the time to get sick over smokin'." She shook her head. "How do you expect to keep goin' when you didn't more than touch your meal tonight?"

He seized the opportunity to get some food for Eb without detection. "Would you fix me a little bread and meat and slip it up to my room later on, Jenny? I'll likely feel better after a while, and I'm goin' to be hungry when I do."

She sighed, but with a certain satisfaction. There was an adventurous streak in Jenny; she would have liked to try smoking herself if she had dared, and she was a little amused that her sober young brother had been tempted in this direction of most young males.

Jethro lay awake in his room that night and wrestled with his problem. He wondered if, after all, it wouldn't be better to ask his father's advice, but he decided against that almost immediately and as firmly as he had rejected the idea that afternoon. He wondered about Ross Milton, but there was little chance to make a trip to Newton at this time of year. What about Ed Turner, staunch, levelheaded neighbor? No, Ed had two sons in the army; it wouldn't do to lay this responsibility upon Ed's shoulders. He thought of Eb's words, "You ner no one else kin help me now—not even Ol' Abe hisself."

Ol' Abe. Mr. Lincoln. Mr. President. Not even Mr. Lincoln himself!

Jethro turned restlessly in his bed. What if one put it up to Mr. Lincoln? What if one said, "I will abide by the word of him who is highest in this land"? But wasn't that word already known? Wasn't the word from the highest in the land just this: turn in deserters or there will be terrible trouble for you and your family?

But Mr. Lincoln was a man who looked at problems from all sides. Mr. Lincoln was not a faraway man like General McClellan or Senator Sumner or Secretary of State Seward. Mr. Lincoln had plowed fields in Illinois; he had thought of the problems men came up against; he was not ready to say, "Everything on this side of the line is right, and everything on the other side is wrong."

But would one dare? A nobody, a boy on a southern Illinois farm—would he dare? Mr. Lincoln held the highest office in the land; what would he think? Would it vex him that a boy from southern Illinois could be so bold? And anyway, how could one say it? What manner of words could one use so as not to be too forward, too lacking in respect toward the President of the United States?

Jeth realized he was not going to be able to go to sleep. There was a candle in his room; there was some ink and an old pen that Bill had sometimes used. There was also Ross Milton's book—the book on English usage. Jethro got up in the quiet of the night, lighted his candle, opened Ross Milton's book, and began to write on a piece of rough lined paper.

The next morning he hid Jenny's sandwiches inside his coat, and at the barn he picked up a few eggs from the nests up in the loft. He dug an apple out of the straw in the apple-cave; no one would question that—a boy needed something to munch on in midmorning. He would like to have taken some coffee beans—a man lying out in the woods all night needed a hot drink; but that item was one he would not take. Not for Eb, not even for Bill or Shad, would he have taken his mother's coffee. He knew where there were good sassafras roots in the woods; maybe he would burn some brush in the fencerows and heat a little water for sassafras tea. He filched an old kettle and two lumps of sugar, just in case.

Eb was feeling a little better that morning. The quilts Jethro had taken from Nancy's house had made the long night more comfortable; he had washed himself in the creek and looked refreshed.

"You've brung me a feast, Jeth," he said gratefully.

They sat together for a while and talked in low voices.

"I'll be gittin' out in a day or so, Jeth. I caint hev you takin' all this risk."

"If you could go back to the army, you would, wouldn't you, Eb?"

"You're askin' a man if he had a chancet to live, would he take it. But I've told you, Jeth—a deserter caint go back. I'll be hunted the rest of my days—but the rest of my days ain't goin' to be too many."

Jethro said nothing, but as he plowed that morning he made up his mind to send the letter. It was a frightening thing to do, but if one did nothing—well, that was frightening too. He knew Eb was not really planning to leave—Eb was a lost and frightened boy, and there was nowhere else to go. For Jethro there was nothing to do but send the letter.

The plowshares needed sharpening, Jethro told his father that noon. Hadn't he better drive over to Hidalgo and get that work done? He'd pick up the mail, too, for themselves and for Ed Turner. Was that all right with his father?

Matt seldom questioned Jethro's decisions. The boy was doing a man's work; he was due the dignity accorded to a man. Matt assented to the trip readily, and Jethro, with the letter in his pocket, drove off down the road, his heart pounding with excitement.

In Hidalgo the old man who took care of the mail glanced sharply at Jethro when he noticed the inscription on the envelope. But he was a silent man with problems of his own; as long as a letter was properly stamped and addressed it was no affair of his. Privately he thought that some people were allowing their young ones to become a little forward, but that was their concern. He threw Jethro's letter in a big bag that would be taken by wagon down to Olney that evening.

The long wait for an answer was interminable. Jethro tossed at night and wondered: had he done an impudent thing, had he laid himself open to trouble, had he been a fool to think that a boy of his age might act without the advice of his elders? Sometimes he got up and walked about his narrow room, but that was bad, for Jenny would hear him. Once she came to his door, and she was crying.

"Jeth—Jeth, what is it? What's botherin' you? Ain't we good friends anymore, ain't you goin' to tell me?"

He had to be curt with her to forestall any more questions. After that she didn't come to his door again, but he knew that if he stirred or moaned under his burden of worry, both Jenny and Nancy would hear him and worry through a sleepless night.

Eb's often reiterated, "I'll be goin' on soon, Jeth; I won't be a burden to you much longer," became like the whippoorwill's cry—always the same and never ending. Jethro closed his ears to it, but the tensions within him mounted, and the necessity of providing for Eb's needs in strictest secrecy became a task that seemed to grow in magnitude as the days went by.

"If I could be sure I'm doin' the right thing," he would say to himself, as he watched the dark earth fall away from his plowshares. "If I could feel really set-up about doin' a fine thing, but I don't know. Maybe I'm doin' somethin' terrible wrong; maybe the next time they come, the Federal Registrars will take me."

The letter came one noon when they were all seated at dinner. As so often happened, it was Ed Turner who brought the mail out from town. Jenny ran to the door, eager for a letter from Shadrach; Nancy's eyes pleaded for word from John.

But Ed held only one large envelope, and that was addressed to Jethro in a small, cramped handwriting done in very black ink. It was postmarked Washington, D.C.

"Looks like purty important mail you're gittin', Jethro," Ed said quietly. His eyes were full of puzzled concern.

Jethro's head swam. This was the showdown; now, all the family, Ed Turner, and soon the neighborhood would know everything. In the few seconds that passed before he opened the envelope, he wished with all his heart that he had not meddled in the affairs of a country at war, that he had let Eb work out his own problems, that he, Jethro, were still a sheltered young boy who did the tasks his father set for him and shunned the idea that he dare think for himself. He looked at the faces around him, and they spun in a strange mist of color—black eyes and blue eyes, gray hair and gold and black, pink cheeks and pale ones and weather-beaten brown ones.

He read the letter through, word for word, and while he read, there wasn't a sound in the cabin beyond the slight rustle of the page in the shaking hand that held it. When he was through, he held the letter out to Jenny, with a long sigh.

"You can read it out loud, Jenny."

Jenny stared at him as if he were a stranger; then she shook her head.

"It's your letter, Jeth; you'd best do the readin'."

He didn't know whether he could or not—there was a great pounding in his ears and his breath was short—but he ran his hand across his eyes and swallowed hard. After the first few words, his voice grew steady, and he read the letter through without faltering.

Executive Mansion
March 14, 1863

Master Jethro Creighton
Hidalgo, Illinois

Dear Jethro:
    Mr. Hay has called my attention to
your letter, knowing as he does the place in

my affection for boys of your age and the interest I have in letters coming from my home state of Illinois.

The problem which you describe is one, among so many others, that has troubled both my waking thoughts and those that intrude upon my sleep. The gravity of that problem has become of far-reaching significance and is one in which the authority of military regulations, the decline of moral responsibility, and the question of ordinary human compassion are so involved as to present a situation in which a solution becomes agonizingly difficult.

I had, however, made a decision relative to this problem only a few days before receiving your letter. There will be much criticism of that decision, but you will understand when I say if it be a wrong one, I have then erred on the side of mercy.

The conditions of that decision are as follows: all soldiers improperly absent from their posts, who will report at certain points designated by local recruit offices by April 1, will be restored to their respective regiments without punishment except for forfeiture of pay and allowances for the period of their absence.

This information you may relay to the young man in question, and I pray that the remorse and despair which he has known since the time of his desertion will bring his better self to the cause for which so many of his young compatriots have laid down their lives.

May God bless you for the earnestness with which you have tried to seek out what is right; may He guide both of us in that search during the days ahead of us.

Yours, very sincerely and respectfully,
Abraham Lincoln

Chapter 10

IN May of 1863 news came from the East of another Union disaster, this time at Chancellorsville. It was frightening news for, whatever one wished to believe, the very obvious fact was that a Union army with the advantage of greatly superior numbers had been terribly beaten by a Confederate army with the advantage of a greatly superior general. The contrast between Robert E. Lee and Joseph Hooker was not one to bring either pride or hope to the Union cause.

The papers had carried stories and pictures of Joseph Hooker all during the winter of '62-'63. He was a tall, handsome man with wavy blond hair and the look of a daredevil in his eyes. He was a hard drinker and a hard fighter. "Fighting Joe Hooker" he was called, an arrogant man, highly contemptuous of McClellan and Burnside, of the Confederate Army, and of the possibility of his own defeat. Here was a dashing, fighting, confident man, the papers had said, the kind of general the North so desperately needed. And so he replaced Ambrose Burnside as Commander of the Army of the Potomac. Then there was Chancellorsville, where handsome Joe Hooker folded helplessly before Lee's onslaught, and in the early summer of '63, papers that had expressed admiration for his spirit and confidence were screaming for his head.

But the fall of General Hooker was of little importance compared to the fact that seventeen thousand Union soldiers had gone either to their deaths or to a Confederate prison camp as a result of the battle at Chancellorsville. The same old fear haunted Jethro and his sister, as they silently plowed the young corn during the weeks when more stories of the disaster came with each newspaper: was Shadrach Yale one of the seventeen thousand?

But in late June a letter came from Shadrach, a letter which reflected the deep gloom that hung over the Army of the Potomac, and the anger felt—not only by the common soldier, but by many of the generals—for the kind of leadership Fighting Joe Hooker had exhibited.

There was awe, too, in Shadrach's realization that once more a freak of chance had allowed him to come through alive, but there was no optimism in his hope for future battles.

> *I have been through Antietam, Fredericksburg, and Chancellorsville, hurt only by the agony of others, but there will be more battles, and you must tell yourself sternly, Jenny, that your love for me is no more sacred than the loves for which thousands upon thousands of women are weeping today. I think it wrong that I write to you with hope and optimism for our future; I think I must prepare you for the possibility—no, the probability—of heartbreak. When a man has looked upon such massive waste of life as I have witnessed in these three battles, the presumption to consider his own little personal dreams becomes a matter of supreme egotism.*

A letter from John was more cheerful. The Army of the Cumberland was on the march with General Rosecrans; for weeks they had been drilling, but now they were sure that action was about to begin. There was Confederate General Bragg in Tennessee, who must face "Old Rosy" before the snows fell. Most of the letter, though, was not about armies or campaigns, but of home, of Jethro's letter from the President, of Eb's behavior; there were long paragraphs in which John wanted to know how Nancy was faring, if she was well, how much the little boys had grown, whether or not they remembered their pa. It was a good letter; Nancy read it to the family and over again to Ellen, whose lips moved while she listened as if she were trying to memorize each word.

Eb wrote to Jethro from Mississippi. He was on a river called the Yazoo, not far from Vicksburg, digging ditches, chopping wood, and building bridges. The heat and the dirt were bad, he said, and there was an added hardness to his life brought on by his weeks of "improper absence," but Eb accepted it with humility.

> *Its hard to have sum fellers hate you fer what you done but the blame is mine and Ill take what they say to me and do my job till I fall over.*

Eb thought the Confederate General Pemberton, up in Vicksburg, was beginning to sweat, and that was fine—but the mosquitoes were awful, and lots of the boys were sick with malaria.

The papers had much to say of the operation around Vicksburg. What was Grant doing down there, editors wanted to know. Was he going to continue stumbling all around the country, hesitating, bumbling, waiting week after week with an army mired down in disease-infested marshes?

The men who wrote for the newspapers that Jenny and Jethro read aloud at night did not believe the Confederate Pemberton was "beginning to sweat"; Vicksburg, perched high on the bluffs of the Mississippi, had a natural fortification that Grant, with his inept stupidity, could not successfully storm any sooner than Joe Hooker could overtake Robert E. Lee.

It was known that the President was being besieged to get rid of Grant. After all, wasn't it true that it was not Grant who had been the victor at Fort Henry, but Admiral Foote and his ironclads? And on second thought, white-haired old C. F. Smith had actually been the brain behind the victory at Donelson. Nobody could deny that Grant had waited too long and had been surprised at Pittsburg Landing, and certainly he had been driven back at Oxford, Mississippi. And in all these stories came the vague charges of drunkenness on the part of the discredited general. The stories were never verified, but they occurred often enough to arouse deep anger in the minds of people whose sons had died under Grant's command. Ellen and Matt felt that anger; for many months neither Jethro nor Jenny ever mentioned Grant before their parents.

Despite the pressures, though, the President did not remove General Grant. But Joseph Hooker was removed—another one of the President's generals acknowledged as a failure in the command of the Army of the Potomac. Now, a new name came more fully into the public eye: George Gordon Meade. The men who came of a Sunday afternoon to talk of the war with Matt wondered how long this new general would last.

The news, however, that overshadowed everything else during that June was the activity of Robert E.

Lee. He had turned away from Richmond, and now, for the first time during the war, a Confederate army was penetrating into the North, into Shadrach's home state of Pennsylvania. There were many speculations: if Lee should take the cities of Harrisburg and Philadelphia, might he not go on to Baltimore and then to Washington? Did Lee plan to let Richmond fall and in its stead to seize Washington—wouldn't the exchange of capitals be worth his while? And weren't the chances for his success a good deal more than fair? This man, Lee, had become a legend, a fearful one for the North. Would it ever be possible to defeat him? The results of some battles had been a draw, but were they ever a real defeat? The new general, Meade, had never had the experience of planning a campaign or of handling a huge army drawn up into battle; Robert E. Lee had little to fear as he maneuvered his army into Pennsylvania.

Out of the gloom of these predictions came the news during early July of Gettysburg, a spot of ground in Pennsylvania that Jethro had never heard of before. The news of the battle was confused at first, incoherent, sometimes contradictory, but one thing was certain: here was a clash that roared with a violence and terror such as the country had never known. It was a battle of unbelievable bravery and unbelievable ruthlessness; it was a clash of agonizing errors checkered with moves of brilliant strategy that lasted through three hot July days, after which the news of victory came: a Union victory and a great one, but still not a complete one. With broken young bodies piled high at Gettysburg and thousands of homes rocked in agony over their loss, the beaten army was allowed to withdraw and prepare for still more bloodshed, while the victorious army licked its wounds and made no effort to pursue its opportunities. All over the North people were beginning to say, "What is it—what does it mean? Is there bad blood somewhere? Is there a conspiracy among Northern generals that prevents their following up an opportunity for crushing Lee's army?"

Then in the midst of the pandemonium over Gettysburg another Union victory was announced: Vicksburg had fallen! General Pemberton, completely surrounded by Grant's army, had been cut off from all supplies and had been starved into surrender. Grant was a hero once again in the papers that had printed no good word of him in months; Ulysses S. Grant was the man of the hour, and some people with short memories said, "I told you so—old Unconditional Surrender Grant is the man who will win this war. Abe Lincoln was right; they'd better send a barrel of the liquor Grant drinks to some of his other generals. God bless old U.S. Grant!"

Of the fall of Vicksburg the President said, "The Father of Waters again goes unvexed to the Sea." Jethro smiled as he read that. What he would give to talk to Shad about those words of Mr. Lincoln's, to remember with him that night when they had looked at the long wavy line on a roughly drawn map and had wondered how long the fighting would go on.

Shadrach, however, was very far away and was a part of the price which the battle of Gettysburg had cost. A letter came addressed to Matt from a spinster aunt of Shadrach's who lived in Washington, a woman of whom Shad had often spoken. The letter ran in part:

> . . . . *He was brought here from Gettysburg with serious wounds which*

became gangrenous before his arrival. I was fortunate in finding him since I am a volunteer nurse at the hospital where he lies. He has had short periods of consciousness during which time he has begged me to write to Jenny Creighton—he calls for her constantly in his delirium. I wish to tell you, sir, that I will gladly pay the girl's expenses to Washington and give her shelter in my home if you will allow her to make the trip. . . . I must tell you that my nephew's condition is very critical. . . .

Ross Milton had driven up to the farm the day the letter came. The editor was often a visitor, spending hours talking to Matt, staying overnight now and then, and testing Jethro's progess in the book on English usage. Sometimes Jenny would join in taking the tests, and Ross Milton would tease her a little: "The wife of a schoolmaster must learn to speak correctly, mustn't she, Jenny?" The family was always glad to see him; he enlivened for a short time the passing of one monotonous day after another.

Later, on the day the news came from Shadrach's aunt, Jethro sat with his father and the editor in the yard just outside the cabin door. The hot summer night was velvet black across the fields and in the dooryard too, except for a ray of lamplight that came from the room where Ellen and Nancy sat beside Jenny and tried to comfort her. The three who sat in the dooryard did not speak; there was no sound in the night except for the deep, tired sobs within the cabin.

Finally Ross Milton leaned forward in his chair. "Matt," he said in a low voice, "if you will let her go to him, I'll take her to Washington and see that she is safe."

For a while Jethro thought that his father was never going to reply. The old man sat turning his cane between his hands and staring down in the darkness at his feet.

Finally he said, "Ain't it ten to one that it's too late?"

"As I see it, you'd better gamble, Matt. It will be better for the girl to have tried to get to him even if it *is* too late. And if it's not too late—I'm a hard-bitten bachelor, Matt, but I don't underestimate the possibilities of young love in a situation like this."

"I kin pay my own girl's expense; I'll not hev her beholden to a stranger. But what about you, Milton? You ain't in health fer the likes of that journey, air you?"

"I can clench my teeth against pain in a railway car as well as at home. I'll go with her if you say the word."

"I wouldn't let them marry," Matt said slowly. "I thought she was too young—and so she is. Still, a man don't allus know what's best. I only know I can't stand to see her suffer this way if there be one chance fer her to see him alive." He reached out to Jethro then for aid in helping him to rise. "I'll hev to talk with Ellen," he said. "Let's go inside."

It was all arranged that night, and the next morning, when Jethro awoke and went downstairs at dawn, he found Jenny already dressed in her best clothes, her face wan and pale, but her weeping stopped by excitement and a thin hope. She put her arms around her brother, and Jethro returned her embrace. They didn't say anything; there was too much danger of a breakdown if they talked.

An hour later Jenny and Ross Milton were gone in the buggy he had driven up from Newton. They would go to Olney, take the train to St. Louis, and from there go on to Washington.

Jethro did not go to the fields that day; instead he roamed about and finally, as if drawn to it, went up to the room adjoining the schoolhouse—the room Matt Creighton had allowed to be built because "a man has the right to his own fireside after a hard day's work."

The room had been used the winter before by a teacher who had been hired for the three winter months, a term during which Jethro had gone to school for only a few days. The elderly teacher was a man without learning, without the wisdom that some unlearned men acquire with their years, without even the saving grace of kindness. Remembering the wonder and pleasure of learning when Shadrach taught, Jethro walked away from the classroom with fierce resentment.

"I get more out of staying home and reading the newspapers—the way Shad told me to do—and working out the exercises in Mr. Milton's book," he told his father.

There had been a time when Matt Creighton brooked no criticism of a teacher from his children; they went to school when it was in session, the teacher's word was law, and their father wanted to hear no complaints concerning either discipline or the quality of instruction. But Matt had changed in his later years. He talked to the teacher for a while one afternoon; that night he gave Jethro permission to remain at home.

"The man is not only without book-larnin', as I am, but he has a mean and pinched-in mind," Matt told Ellen. "The boy is right; he'll larn more by tenfold on his own."

As Jethro looked about the room that morning of

Jenny's departure, he felt a dull anger at sight of the cluttered filth the old teacher had left. The room had once been a place of beauty for Jethro, a room of color and firelight, of books and singing and a sense of deep friendship, which he was sure he would never have again if Shadrach died in the Washington hospital. He touched the roughhewn bookshelves, the mantel above the fireplace, the wall where the guitar had hung.

"Maybe I'll ask Nancy for soap and water; maybe she'll help me clean the place," he whispered to himself. "If Shad ever comes back, I'd like for this room to be clean and nice for him."

Then he shook his head at his own dreaming. He had heard Ross Milton warning Jenny the night before, "We must remember, girl, that there's only one chance in a hundred that this trip will have a happy ending. But we're going to concentrate on that one chance."

Jethro sat down on a bench in the hot, dusty room; there was no comfort in being there, but he could think of no other place where he wished to be.

They lived through many dreary days of waiting. Every day someone—Nancy and Jethro, Ed Turner, even Matt when the others were too busy—would drive into town to see if there was a letter. For many days there wasn't, and the only slim comfort they could find was to remember that there was one chance—one in maybe a hundred.

Then finally there came a letter from Ross Milton.

. . . . The boy is still desperately ill, but he will live—I am convinced of that, in spite of all my fears, for if ever a lad seized life and held onto it with both hands, it was young Yale who did so when he

opened his eyes and saw that little girl you
had sent to him. . . .

There were many letters from both Jenny and Ross
Milton that summer, letters that brought hope and
comfort to the family at home.

> *. . . . The long ride on the trains was*
> *like a bad dream to me," the first letter*
> *from Jenny ran, "but Mr. Milton talked to*
> *me with the greatest kindness and he kept*
> *my spirits up. When finly we got here I was*
> *so tired and my dress was wrinkled and full*
> *of dust but the minute I saw Shad it was*
> *like heaven for both of us. I thank you pa*
> *and ma, and I will thank you all the days*
> *of my life that you let me come to him. I*
> *feel sure that you have saved his life and*
> *my happyness. . . .*

Later there came a request from the young
couple, a request written and subscribed to by a
hard-bitten bachelor, Ross Milton. Matt dictated
his answer to Jethro and then signed his own
trembling signature.

> *My wife and I give consent that our*
> *daughter Jenny Elizabeth Creighton, age*
> *16, may marry Shadrach Yale, Union*
> *soldier, under the witness of a trusted*
> *friend, Editor Ross Milton.*
> *Signed: Matthew Benjamin Creighton*

The envelope carrying Jenny's next letter bore
a self-conscious return address in the upper left-
hand corner, a return to *Mrs.* Shadrach Yale of

Washington, D. C. The first paragraph of the letter within that envelope was addressed to Jethro:

> . . . *and please take down the Bible, Jeth, and in your best hand write this beside my name—Married to Shadrach Yale, August 14, 1863.*

Then she went on to describe her wedding day:

> . . . . *I wore the white dress you give me in the kindness of your heart Nancy, and it was washed and ironed fresh and pretty. Mr. Milton went out and bought the ring for Shad. It is solid gold, and it has little lines in it that make it look like gold lace. I think I will never take it off. I stood by Shads bed, and there was sick boys all around, but they all smiled at me. So did Aunt Victoria who doesnt smile very offen, poor woman, because she works so hard and sees so much of suffering. Mr. Milton had to leave right away to take the train back home, but he kissed my hand before he left and called me Mrs. Yale, and that sounded so nice to me. The only thing that could of been better was if all of you that I love so much had been here. . . .*

She told of her life as a young bride in Washington in another letter:

> *I go to the hospital every day and do all I can to ease the pain that is all around me. At first Aunt Victoria said it wasnt right for a young girl to be here, but I made her*

see that I couldnt set at home when others was needing help so much. I do what the nurses tell me and they say I mind them and dont make trubel like some ladys do here. Some of the things I see would of made me faint a year ago, but now I face them the way the nurses and doctors do. I do all I can to help others because I thank God so much that Shad is going to get well.

Aunt Victoria has a nice big house with a real stove in the kitchen. She lets me make big kettels of soup there, and a man she knows comes and takes it to the hospital in a little wagon. I feed as many boys as I can from it because they sometimes have to eat stuff that we would throw away at home. Sometimes I bake fresh bread and spread it with butter, and Shad and them that is laying near him clap there hands when they see me begin to hand it out.

It is hot in this city, and sometimes at night when I come back to Aunt Victorias house I am tired and wishful for the silver poplars to set under. I see all your faces in my mind, and I wonder how is Jeth getting along in the fields by himself, and I think how good it is that Nancy and the little boys are there to give you comfort. There is so much pain and sorrow here. And the city is bad to. There is filth in the streets and flys swarming and even rats running sometimes right in front of me when I walk home. But this is where my husband is and I wouldnt want to be anywhere in this world except close by his side. But

sometimes I wonder if we are the only two
happy people in this town. . . .

Jethro took the letters after the others had finished reading them and kept them in his room, where he could read and reread them to himself. He felt a great sense of peace within him as he read. Shad was going to live! Over and over he repeated those words, and in the morning when he woke with a feeling of happiness and wondered at the cause of it, he would remember—Shad was going to live! He felt as if somehow he had been granted a gift in escaping a sorrow that would have scarred his life.

The letter he finally wrote to Jenny with Ross Milton's book close at hand as an aid to spelling was a simple one. He had no fine phrases to help him convey his feelings; but Jenny found it a good letter, and she kept it all the years of her life.

> *Dear Jenny,*
>   *We are all feeling much pleasure here to know that Shad is better and is going to get well. We are glad that you and Shad are married. It is hard to get used to thinking that you are Mrs. Yale and not just Jenny. If only the war would soon be over and you and Shad could come back here it would be a wonderful happy thing for all of us. The crops are good but we could use some rain. Your pa and ma are well as usual and your sister Nancy is to. The little boys are in good health except that Johnny run a nail in his foot last week but he is allrite now. It is lonesome to work in the fields without you to talk to and to make me laugh sometimes. But it is beter for you*

*to be with Shad. I wrote what you told me
to in the Bible and it looks fine. Do you
ever see Mr. Lincoln? I would like to see
him very much and thank him for the letter
he wrote to me. What does Shad think
about it that General Grant is the top man
in the army now? You ask him for me.*

  Yours very truly,
  Your brother Jethro H. Creighton

Chapter 11

NANCY had heard from John in June; it was a long time before she heard from him again—early December of 1863. He wrote a long letter then; he had a long story to tell. He began:

I gess you heered about Chickamauga.

During the dreary days in which she had heard nothing from her husband, the name Chickamauga had held desolation and despair for Nancy. She had studied the newspaper map with Jethro, the map of Chattanooga down on the Tennessee River, with Lookout Mountain to the southwest, Missionary Ridge facing on the east, and beyond the Ridge, the line of water labelled "Chickamauga Creek." The newspaper accounts were hard for both her and Jethro to understand; they were stories of chaotic confusion, of bitter fighting and terrible disaster. In September of 1863, the Army of the Cumberland had finally encountered General Bragg, who was soon reinforced by General Longstreet. The Confederates thus outnumbered Rosecrans' army by as many as twenty thousand, and they handed a terrible defeat to the army that had so cheerfully set out upon its march in June. A terrible defeat, but not quite a complete one, for the left wing of the Army of the Cumberland had held firm under the command of a general named George Thomas.

There were many names in the papers those days—names of men and places that for a time were on everybody's tongue and then quite often were almost forgotten, while other names gained prominence in the news. The name George Thomas had been a great one at Logan's Crossroads, when the big Virginian who had decided to remain loyal to the Union had given the Federals their first taste of victory in the West. But that had been before Donelson, and for Jethro, the meaning of the war began with Donelson. Thus he had failed to identify the name of Thomas at first, but after September of 1863 it would never again be either ignored or forgotten by Jethro or by anyone of his time for whom the news of the war mattered. "The Rock of Chickamauga," the papers called him, after the soldiers under his command had held out against twice their number with a stubbornness that finally forced Bragg to give up, thus leaving Thomas and his men free to go back to Chattanooga.

Other names prominent in that battle were, true to the temper of the times, disgraced and dragged through the mud. Those who fought battles comfortably within their homes or newspaper offices had more than enough mud to spare. Rosecrans, McCook, and Crittenden, who in the bewildering mountain terrain had completely lost control of the men they were supposed to command, were now accused of everything from downright stupidity to traitorous complicity with the enemy.

After the hope and jubilation that Vicksburg and Gettysburg had inspired in July, Chickamauga was a dreadful reversal for the North to suffer; for Nancy it was a name threatening her with "hard news" until the day John's letter came.

I gess you heered about Chickamauga.
It was somethin we didnt like to think
about. Its a terrble feelin to be beat and tho

some of our boys held out with Gen Thomas the most of us was ashamed and licked. But now I am goin to tell you another story and Im proud of this one. You tell Jeth to save all the papers about this battel that Im tellin you about. When I come home Ill read em and tell you if they be rite. . . .

After that, John's letter was a long narrative of what had happened in the mountains around Chattanooga during that cold November of '63. Jethro had read accounts of it in the papers, but John's story was closer, more immediate. It was a vivid picture, and as Jethro read, he felt as if he were an actual witness to the unbelievable thing that had happened.

John wrote of how near the army had been to starvation after Chickamauga; how the snipers located all along the slopes of Lookout Mountain and Missionary Ridge made it impossible for a wagonload of food or provender to get through to either men or animals.

. . . . We et things that wood make you sick to think about and the pore horses and mules was as despert hongry as we was. . . .

Then he told of the reinforcements that arrived: Joseph Hooker with detachments from the Army of the Potomac; William Tecumseh Sherman with most of the Army of the Tennessee. And Grant came down in person, Grant with his new promotion that placed him over Hooker, Sherman, Rosecrans, Thomas, and the others in the West.

. . . . It didnt set good with us, these other armys comin in to help us out. The Army of the Cumberland hadnt done so bad in days gone by, we wasnt licked at Stones River. We didnt like the way they peered to look down on us. The Potomac boys are mitey hifalutin, some of em, and they and the Tennessee boys and us pure hated each other worse than we hated the rebs. . . .

The next paragraphs explained Grant's strategy of the battle: Hooker would strike at one end of the Confederate line on Lookout Mountain; Sherman would hit the other end on Missionary Ridge. The Army of the Cumberland would attack the center—an easier job, John said, because they were only expected to worry Bragg enough to keep him from sending men from his center to reinforce his ends.

. . . . It aint that we was so much apantin to fite, wed had aplenty of fitin. Still we didnt like it of Grant to give us the easy post and hev the Potomac and Tennessee boys lookin at us like we was a third rate army. If youve read of Hookers boys afitin the battel up on Lookout you kno that it was fine. They licked the rebs up ther and we had to admit that they done what we hadnt. But you shood a seen Joe Hooker strut. . . .

John went on to say that things weren't going so well with Sherman's men, and the Cumberland boys waited with excitement mounting by the minute. Then finally the command came for them to take the front-line trenches at the base of Missionary Ridge, which towered like a steep wall opposite Lookout. That was when pandemonium broke out!

> . . . .*We wanted to pitch in like we had never wanted to before. We must of bin a littel crazy becus we didnt stop with the first-line trenches but we started up the slope of the old Ridge and ther was yellin and screechin like I hev never heered. Ther was officers alookin fine in ther best uniforms and they went yellin with us. There was a short littel Irish officer named Sheridan and he took hisself a drink and shook the bottle at the rebs and went yellin up that slope like he didnt care was he an officer or not. It got to be a race to see what regiment would make it to the top first and I want you to kno that old 104th Illinois didnt do so bad. And the rebs I gess thot we was teched and they begin to give way. After that the center of Braggs line cracked all to peeces. I dont kno what the papers said but I want you to kno that it was the Army of the Cumberland that done it. . . .*

Jethro rewrote John's letter carefully and sent his copy to Shadrach and Jenny in Washington. He made mountains of chips and stones out in the wood lot and showed John's little boys how their father, along with the boys in the Army of the Cumberland, had scaled Missionary Ridge and had so broken the center of the Confederate line that General Bragg had had to order his divided army to retreat and to leave Chattanooga in the hands of the Federals.

Nancy wrote to John of Jethro's interest in his description of the battle, and weeks later John spoke of it in his reply:

> . . . . *What you told me about Jeths intrust made good readin. And it brings comfert to me that the one brother Ive got left is close to my littel boys. . . .*

In November of that year the President made a speech at Gettysburg; papers all over the country printed it, but they were not agreed upon its quality. One of the papers Jethro read claimed that "the cheek of every American must tingle with shame at the silly, flat, dish-watery utterances." Another said that the President's speech would live among the annals of man. Jethro didn't know. He loved Mr. Lincoln and felt deeply drawn to him; it angered him to read the mouthings of hate directed toward the President, but as to whether the address at Gettysburg was a great one or just another speech, an eleven-year-old farm boy did not know. He read it aloud to his mother.

"It has the ring of the Scriptures about it, Jeth," she said.

He nodded. It had, somewhat, he thought.

That winter many people were talking of peace. The end could not be rushed; there would be fighting to the last ditch, but the end was inevitable. A people pushed to the extremities that existed in the South could not possibly hold on, the papers claimed. But they did hold on, and as the war trailed drearily on, vindictiveness toward the stubborn stand of the seceding states grew steadily more bitter in the North. This vindictiveness was urged on by men in high places who resented the President's spirit of clemency as violently as they resented the tenacity of the South.

In December Abraham Lincoln issued a proclamation of amnesty, in which he promised pardon and full rights to any individual Confederate who would swear to protect the Constitution and the Union of the states, to abide by the government's pronouncements against slavery. He promised, too, that a Confederate state could return to the Union whenever ten per cent of its voters should reestablish a loyal Union government within that state.

"Never hev I loved him so much," Matt exclaimed tearfully. And Jethro remembered words in the President's letter: "There will be much criticism, but if I err it will be on the side of mercy."

The criticism of his act came with quick violence from all sections of the country. In the South the Confederate Congress cried out that if the Washington government called for restoration of the Union it was merely setting a cruel trap for the deluded; that it would be only a relationship between the conqueror and the conquered; that it would mean personal and public degradation and ruin. And in the North the chant of hate against Lincoln became stronger than ever. His proclamation of amnesty was little better than treason, the President's detractors shouted, and many people began to consider it high patriotism to talk of the coming wholesale execution of rebels.

The third winter of the war went by with the echoing story of suffering and death. In the early part of the war's fourth year, General Grant was placed in command of all the armies of the United States. With this promotion another general fell to a lower place—General Halleck, who had never quite risen to his position, was finally relegated to the list of those whose names had soared for a while and then fallen into near-obscurity. Jethro could remember the early days of the war when he had felt resentful upon learning that Halleck was Grant's superior officer. In March of 1864 he felt a glow of personal triumph that his resentment had perhaps been justified.

In Washington, Shadrach Yale was slowly struggling back to health in the safety of his aunt's home. Now that Jenny was with him, Shad's letters were addressed to Jethro. They were like gifts to the lonely boy; he read them over again and again, and then placed them carefully in the big envelope containing the President's letter.

Shadrach wrote that he and Jenny had seen the President and General Grant as they drove through the Washington streets together.

> . . . . *The President's face is deeply lined, and his cheeks are gaunt. I have seen so many soldiers whose cheeks have had that sunken look, even though they were young faces. . . . The President looks at least twenty years older than the pictures you and I used to study together in the early days of the war. But his face was full of light as the crowds cheered; I think he knew they were cheering Grant and that pleased him, for I'd guess that he, too, wanted to cheer the little man who sat beside him.*
>
> *Grant does not have the appearance of a great general; he looks awkward, ill at ease, and carelessly dressed. But we have had enough of charm and polish; this commander who doesn't even walk like a military man is the one who will, I believe, restore the Union. . . .*

Early in 1864 talk of the presidential election was in the air. Jethro had been barely conscious of the excitement, anger, and vicious invective that had accompanied the election of 1860; now he was fully conscious of emotions of even deeper violence in the talk of men in the community and in the papers that he read.

There was hatred for Mr. Lincoln within his own party as well as in the Democratic party. Thad Stevens, the aging floor leader in the House of Representatives, pushed his program of "no mercy to the South" and let his contempt for the President spill out in every speech he made. Midwestern newspapers reprinted the blasts of Wendell Phillips in the East, and of Editor Horace Greeley, who asked rhetorically if this man Lincoln was the sole hope of the Republican Party. The answer, he thundered, was in the negative: did not such men as General Frémont, General Wade Butler, General Ulysses S. Grant, rank high above Abraham Lincoln?

The Democratic Party's strongest asset lay in the weariness of war throughout the country. Men lost were no longer counted by the thousands but by the hundred thousands; there had been blundering, betrayal, and corruption during the entire progress of the war. There was fierce resentment among many when the President and the Secretary of War used every resource at their hands to raise more troops to support Grant and Sherman. And with all these angers there was an added agony when hopes for an end to the war were crushed as the year progressed.

The country had waited expectantly that summer to hear of a decisive victory by its hero-commander, Grant. Instead, news came of the Battle of the Wilderness, a horrifying story of fighting in a blazing woods, with losses mounting by the thousands and with Lee still holding firm. It had the sound of Fredericksburg and Chancellorsville all over again.

Soldiers of the Army of the Potomac, loyal still to McClellan, had nodded cynically at the advent of Grant. "Sure," they said, "Grant looked pretty good in the West, but remember that out West he hadn't met up with Bobby E. Lee."

Now, in the Battle of the Wilderness, and later for a full month of fighting at a place called Spotsylvania and along the Chickahominy River, and finally at a blazing crossroads known as Cold Harbor, Grant had met Robert E. Lee; and he was no more a conqueror of that legendary general than George B. McClellan had been. There was one difference though: Grant would not give up. He gave his opponent no quarter, and the stubborn tenacity with which he held on in the face of Lee's punishment was something the soldiers of the Army of the Potomac had never seen in their idolized General McClellan.

But, for all of Grant's determination, the North appeared to be no nearer victory than it had been before the fury and waves of death had begun the month before. He had, however, managed to get away from Lee and, moving south, had come up to the town of Petersburg. At that, Northern papers took hope and began shouting. Through Petersburg ran the railroads by which Lee's army received its supplies; if Petersburg were taken, then the cry of "On to Richmond" would at last be fulfilled.

Jubilantly the news came: Petersburg was in Grant's hands! Then a retraction: Petersburg was not quite in Grant's hands—only the outworks. And finally: a siege would be necessary before the city would be in Grant's hands.

A moan of disappointment and despair went up over the country. The end of the war had appeared to be so near and now, after the horror of the Wilderness and Cold Harbor, there must be a siege of Petersburg. The nation was ready to look for peace. If the price of peace was the dissolution of the Union, many people felt that compensation lay in stopping human slaughter. The Northern Democrats saw their chance.

Lincoln had been nominated in June in spite of the reluctance of the men within his party who hated him. But in late summer with the word of Federal reverses pouring in, many papers shouted that he stood no chance for reelection, and to Jethro it seemed that most men were agreed.

Ross Milton was not, however; he said, "Lincoln will win. When it comes to the final vote, the country will not admit that its sons have died for nothing."

But Matt shook his head. "I want to believe it," he said, "but I don't. I think we're in the midst of an awful crumble."

In Chicago during the month of August, 1864, the Democrats nominated George B. McClellan as their candidate for the presidency. After days in which the Democratic nomination filled the papers, there came suddenly the thunderbolt of General McClellan's response to his nomination. Shadrach wrote of that response to Jethro:

> . . . . *I could not cheer General McClellan at Antietam; I watched the men who had been under his command for months and wondered at the love they felt for this man who, to my way of thinking, had prolonged the suffering and bloodshed of this struggle through some aspect of his nature that lacked, not the courage to face personal danger, but the courage to risk being wrong.*

Today as I read General McClellan's response to the Democratic Committee, so set to elect him as an advocate of their peace platform, I thought that I must write to you and point out a quality of courage in this man that I wouldn't have believed to be there.

I gave a yell when I read it, and your sister was aghast. She said, "But, Shad, I thought you were all for Mr. Lincoln!" and I had to explain to my dearly beloved and legally wed Jenny that I am "all for Mr. Lincoln," but that today I've had to give a belated cheer for my former commander.

Shadrach sent a clipping from a Washington newspaper in case Jethro had missed General McClellan's response. The article quoted the general as saying that as far as he was concerned, the party's platform meant that the North was not to offer peace on any terms short of the reestablishment of the Union, that to accept anything else would be an insult and an affront to the thousands of soldiers who had died in battle. Shadrach added a note at the bottom of the article: "This is the man whom the radical Republicans accused of traitorous disloyalty!"

Then to the sullen and despairing North there came heartening news, the first of which was in a dispatch from Mobile, Alabama. In August, Admiral Farragut had led his fleet in the torpedo-infested waters of Mobile Bay to capture the Confederate *Tennessee,* said to be one of the most powerful warships afloat. After that, land forces had captured three forts guarding the city of Mobile, which meant that the Confederacy had lost its most essential port on the Gulf of Mexico.

In itself the capture of Mobile might not have been a matter of such rejoicing had not other good news arrived upon the heels of it. But in September word came to Washington from the excitable general who, months before, had annoyed Congress with his predictions of a long and difficult war. William Tecumseh Sherman had telegraphed the President that the city of Atlanta, Georgia, had fallen to the Army of the Tennessee.

"Atlanta is ours and fairly won," was Sherman's message to Mr. Lincoln, and that, coupled with the news from Mobile, sent the North into paeans of thanksgiving.

News of victory also came from the Shenandoah Valley, where gallant, steel-nerved Phil Sheridan had defeated the Confederate General Early at Cedar Creek. Sheridan had made a dramatic ride to rally his straggling troops and turn a nearly-lost battle into a decisive Union victory.

The North was still war-weary, but it was no longer hopeless. The prize was almost within its grasp; the goal for which its thousands of boys had died or suffered the agony of prison camps was almost won. It would have been folly to give up with victory so near—so men went to the polls that November and reelected Abraham Lincoln.

The preponderance of the soldier vote was for Lincoln that year. There had been unrest and anger, despair and desertions by the thousands; still, when the vote was taken, the men whose sufferings had been past all belief now took their stand that the war should go on. The news of that vote was heartwarming to the tired President; so, too, was the fact that all the Northern states except Kentucky, Delaware, and New Jersey were of one accord with the soldier vote. That included Mr. Lincoln's home state of Illinois; but to Jethro's disappointment, it was not southern Illinois that gave the state's electoral votes to the President. Even Sangamon County, where Mr. Lincoln had lived all his mature years, gave a plurality of its votes to General George B. McClellan.

After the excitement of the election, the papers began to speculate upon what had become of the Army of the Tennessee. It was lost in a mysterious silence somewhere in Georgia. There were rumors that the Confederate General Hood had encountered Sherman and had cut the Army of the Tennessee to pieces, but they were unconfirmed rumors. When Hood came up from Georgia and through northern Alabama into Tennessee, he did not claim to have defeated Sherman's army.

The Army of the Cumberland was in Tennessee ready to face the same General Hood, and in command of it was "The Rock of Chickamauga," General George Thomas.

Some of Thomas's men had been sent off to the Army of the Tennessee with Sherman. John wrote home that a lot of the boys were behaving like "spoiled young uns," because they believed the Georgia campaign would be a lark with little fighting, while the Army of the Cumberland must stay on to do the stern work of keeping Tennessee in Federal hands.

Perhaps General Hood believed that the Army of the Cumberland, weakened by loss of regiments to the Army of the Tennessee, could be overcome and Tennessee regained for the Confederacy; perhaps he hoped that Sherman would be recalled from Georgia in case General Thomas were too sharply threatened in Tennessee. Whatever the thinking behind the move in this bloody chess game, Hood appeared in

Tennessee in November of 1864, and the two armies clashed at Franklin, only a few miles south of the city of Nashville, where Hood was worsted.

Then came another clash at Nashville in December, and it was from there that John's next letter came. The first page told briefly of the battle:

. . . . *Ther was days of sleet and we coodnt make a move. We set ther waitin and wonderin what was agoin to happen. Then the wether turned warm. As soon as the sleet was melted we started the attack. The fitin was awful bad but Hoods army— what ther was left of it—was druv out of Tennessee and back down to Alabamy. Tell Jeth not to beleve that Grant is the gratest general in this war. I tell you they dont come grater than old Pap Thomas.*

A second sheet was added to this letter, evidently days after the first had been written. It carried news that those at home had almost despaired of hearing.

. . . . *It is late at night but I hev a story to tell and I must rite it becus I cant sleep til I hev told you. A few days ago I was put in charge of helpin to feed the reb prisners that we took in this battel. Tonight when I walked amongst em I seed a man and I swer to you I thot it was pa at first look. The man had a light colered berd like pas was when I was a boy and he had the same blue eyes with pas look in em. I stopt in my tracks and looked agin and then I seed it was my brother Bill growed to look as old as pa looked a fue years back. I didn't dast* to stop or take his hand but I went close and under my breth I told him Id try to come back and I think he nodded but it was so littel that I skarse cood tell he nodded at all. Then I went to my capten and asked him if I cood talk to a reb prisner that was my own blood brother. My capten looked at me. Yore brother he said and then after a long time he said Yes that I cood go ahead.

Wel I found Bill and we set together with thousands of sad men all around us and things was cold and foul everwhere but we was brothers agin and we talked like brothers ought to talk.

He wanted to kno all the news of home and I told him how Tom dide at Pittsburg Landing and of Eb desertin and then goin back. I told him how Jeth had rit a letter to the President and got an anser back. I told him about pas sickness and how my boys was growin up fine with ther good littel ma bringin em up alone. I told him how Shad was near about kilt at Gettysburg and that now him and Jenny was man and wife. All the time his eyes was on the ground and he was sayin nothin but when Id stop hed say tell me more John and Id try to remember more of what was in yore letters. Then come the time when I must go and we shook hands fer a long time like as if our fingers didnt want to let go. And when I turned to go he called me back and he axed me to be shore that I told this to ma and so I am ritin what he said with the hope that it will bring comfort to her. Ma—Bill wants

that I shood tell you this—he was not at
Pittsburg Landing. That bullet was not
fired by him. . . .

Chapter 12

STILL there was no word of Sherman and the lost Army of the Tennessee. All over the country, and in Europe, too, people waited for word as they tried to guess what was happening.

"If he can do it," people said, "if he can march three hundred miles through enemy territory, then it is certain that the Confederacy is nearly spent. If Sherman can do it, then surely the war must be very near its close."

But many remembered that Sherman had always been considered a little "crazy." He looked wild; it was like him to attempt a mad, impossible feat like this.

"But Grant trusts him," some said.

"Yes," replied others, "and Grant has made any number of mistakes, too. He's 'Mr. Big' with Ol' Abe, but that doesn't mean that he's always right."

Suddenly in December the waiting was over, and the Army of the Tennessee was again in contact with Washington.

"I beg to present you the city of Savannah as a Christmas gift," Sherman wired the President.

Quick word followed that the Army of the Tennessee had marched from Atlanta to the sea and had met hardly more than a brush of resistance. It was a signal for great rejoicing in the North.

Then during the next weeks, stories about Sherman's march began filtering back, first to the eastern cities and then to the Midwest. They traveled to the quiet farms, where barns were full of grain and fat stock, where smokehouses were crammed with hams and sides of beef, where apples, cabbages, and potatoes were buried under mounds of earth and straw for winter use, where homes were warm in bitter weather and children slept safely through the nights in feather beds. Out in the Midwest the railroads were intact and carried the farmers' grain and stock to market; trade was good, and prices high. Throughout this part of the country the farms lay tranquil under the winter snow, waiting for spring and the plow and the stir of new life.

People on these farms and in the cities received the stories coming up from Georgia with mixed reactions. The talk among the men who came to visit with Matt at his fireside was all of "Billy Sherman's march through Georgia":

". . . . The Rebs fired on their country's flag. They've held on fer all these months and years, and hundreds of thousands of boys hev been lost to save the Union their great-grandfathers established. Don't talk to me of mercy—Billy Sherman is givin' 'em the mercy they deserve!"

". . . . My boy wrote that it was like a picnic all the way. They et chicken and pork chops and yams every meal if they wanted 'em; they hadn't had grub like that in months. And they burned every fence and house and barn in sight; the railroads they bent up like hairpins—over two hundred miles of 'em."

". . . . A war ain't won that leaves scars like this on folks who be our brothers."

". . . . Hev you heered of Andersonville Prison? Do you know what the Rebs have done in that black hole to *their* brothers?"

"Well, there's Camp Douglas right here in Illinois—hev you heered the stories of *that* place?"

"It's a terr'ble thing, it's a pitiful thing, but it's war. The sooner we make one great swoop, the sooner the sufferin' is over fer all of us—South as well as North."

". . . . There be limits even in war. This was mean, mad destruction. This was war on babies and their mothers, on the sick and old and helpless."

". . . . And they brought it on themselves. They hev to pay the price."

"Would their armies hev spared us if the tables had bin turned? Don't believe it fer one minute!"

Word came that the Army of the Tennessee, after reaching Savannah, had turned north to join Grant; it was then that South Carolina knew the lash of a triumphant army drunk with the plundering of Georgia and enraged at the stubborn tenacity of the South in holding onto a cause that was already lost. In South Carolina the vast, undisciplined army could find another excuse for its excesses beyond the slogan, "This is War, and War is Hell." The role of this state in bringing on the war served as a "just" excuse for atrocities that no thoughtful man could excuse.

"This is the nest where secesh was hatched," the army shouted, and the proud possessions of a gracious life, the little homes of the poor, the cities, farms, and the frightened, desperate people were swept down before the fury of the Army of the Tennessee.

Ed Turner's youngest boy, just eighteen and in the army only a few months, was in South Carolina. Ed brought the boy's letter down for Matt to read. In it the boy told of the burning of Columbia, of how the soldiers laughed as a great wind fanned the flames, of the loot carried off, of mirrors and pianos smashed, and of intimate family treasures scattered to the winds by men who seemed to have gone mad.

Ed Turner's hands trembled as he returned the

letter to its envelope.

"What is this goin' to do to an eighteen-year-old boy, Matt? Kin a lad come through weeks of this kind of actions without becomin' a hardened man? Is human life goin' to be forever cheap to him and decency somethin' to mock at?"

"You and Mary hev larned him right from wrong, Ed."

"But they're bein' cheered on, Matt. Congress—the whole country—is happy with 'em; these boys air goin' to believe that they be heroes fer lootin' and burnin', fer laughin' at distress, fer smashin' the helpless without pity. In some ways Sammy is more of a child than yore Jeth here; he goes with the crowd without thinkin'. Mary and me has had to guard aginst that way of his."

Matt looked at his friend with troubled eyes; any words that he could think of seemed useless, worse than silence.

Ed got to his feet. "Well, it shorely will be over soon. It's got to be over soon. The South can't hold out much longer."

That was what the papers were saying, too, along with the politicians and the men who congregated in little groups at the country stores. Surely it would be over soon. The South was starving, its railroads and seaports gone; Grant was only a few miles from Richmond; Thomas was in Tennessee; and Sherman was roaring up through South Carolina. Any week now, any day, any hour, the great terror that had gripped the land for four years would be over.

Eb wrote from Tennessee. He was with General Schofield's army, and they were marching toward North Carolina to join Sherman when he reached there.

.... Its all goin to be over soon. I figger to be home to help Jeth with the spring plowin and plantin. I hev not felt in sech good spirrits sence the erly days when Tom and me allowed this war was goin to be pure fun. We was like fulish young uns. ...

But the war went on. In Virginia more soldiers died each day in Grant's army and in Lee's because the South, even in its death throes, would not admit defeat, and the tragedy of these deaths was even greater when the hopes of homecoming and peace were just within realization.

Jethro had just turned thirteen in early 1865. He had grown tall during the years of the war, and although he was still slender, there was a taut look about his body, as if all his muscles had attained a fine precision in working together for the achievement of a needed strength. His face was becoming more angular and the great blue eyes of his early years were darkened by shifting lights of gray and green. Matt and Ellen noticed a change in him; he was gentle with them and with Nancy and her children, but there was a reserve about him that had grown steadily greater with the years. They watched him anxiously, wondering and sometimes fearing a little; he was so much like Bill, and Bill, the gentlest of all their sons, had walked out of their lives with a finality that cut like a knife. To lose Jethro would have been too much; unconsciously they clutched at him.

"It's bin long since you hev told me any of the old lessons Shad used to larn you, Jeth," his mother remarked one morning, as she sat before the fire watching him pace aimlessly.

He took a handful of crumbs and tossed them out

to the sparrows that hopped on crusted snowdrifts outside. When he came back he put his hand briefly on her shoulder.

"Seems sometimes that the old lessons are bein' lost in the worry of new things happenin' each day, Ma," he said quietly. "Somehow I don't have the heart for things that used to set me up so much."

"What was on yore mind jest now, Jeth, while you was pacin' back and for'ard?"

"I guess I was thinkin' of some things Mr. Milton said the last time he spent the night with us, things about the war—and peace when it comes."

"Do you want to tell me of 'em? I be proud to hear the things that air in yore mind."

Jethro felt a wrench of pity at her little plea, but he stood before her silent and troubled.

"I can't put it the way Mr. Milton does, Ma," he explained after a while. "I can't make you understand; some things he says I don't quite understand, either. I just have a feelin' for them, and I can't form the thoughts into good words."

Ellen nodded meekly. There were, indeed, many things that she could not understand. Most of Ross Milton's talk was beyond her comprehension. But it was having Jethro talk to her that she wanted, not an understanding of Ross Milton's words.

Jethro walked slowly out of the house. The look in his mother's eyes troubled him; so did the things the editor had talked about on a recent night when he and Jethro sat before the fire in the cabin, after Matt's weariness had forced him off to bed.

"Don't expect peace to be a perfect pearl, Jeth," Ross Milton had warned. "This is a land lying in destruction, physical and spiritual. If the twisted railroads and the burned cities and the fields covered with the bones of dead men—if that were all, we could soon rise out of the destruction. But the hate that burns in old scars, and the thirst for revenge that has distorted men until they should be in straitjackets rather than in high office—these are the things that may make peace a sorry thing. . . ."

Jethro had not liked to hear the editor talk like that. To him peace had been a shining dream, with Shad and Jenny back home, with John more of a brother now and a hero in Jethro's eyes, with Eb coming home in pride instead of degradation. No, of course, peace would not be a perfect pearl, not with young Tom never to return, not with the possibility of Bill's return only the most shadowy and remote of chances. Still, peace would mean a glorious sense of relief; in all his years Jethro had heard either the talk of war's imminence or its reality. He had wished that Ross Milton would not rip up his dream of peace.

He had said to the editor that night: "But we have the President, Mr. Milton. Don't you remember the last of his speech a few weeks ago on Inauguration Day: 'to bind up the nation's wounds, to care for him who should have borne the battle'? Won't the President do away with this hate and revenge that you're tellin' me about?"

Ross Milton had taken a brand from the fireplace carefully between his long fingers, and he waited until he had lighted his pipe before he answered Jethro's question.

"My hope lies in Abraham Lincoln. He has four years before him and the power of a mighty office; if he can control the bigots, if he can allow the defeated their dignity and a chance to rise out of their despair—if he can do this, then maybe peace will not be a mockery."

They had talked of the thirteenth amendment that night. It had been passed by Congress, and now it was up to the states; Illinois had already ratified it—Jethro felt proud that his state was the first to do so—and there was little doubt that three-fourths of the others would follow. Then slavery would be constitutionally abolished once and for all.

"It's a great thing, isn't it, Mr. Milton?"

"It's a far star, Jeth; it's a dim pinpoint of light in the darkness."

Jethro had been provoked. "I don't know why you talk like that," he exclaimed.

The editor reached out and put his hand on Jethro's knee. "Because, Jeth, after the thirteenth amendment has become a part of our Constitution and for years afterward—twenty-five, maybe fifty—there will be men and women with dark faces who will walk the length and width of this land in search of the bright promise the thirteenth amendment holds out to them."

He turned with a sudden thrust of his crippled body to Jethro. "What's going to happen to them, Jeth? What will become of men and women who have known nothing but servitude all the days of their lives? They are without experience, without education; they'll be pawns in the hands of exploiters all over the nation. You watch this thing, Jeth, you watch the abolitionists who have ranted against the South; see if they extend the hand of friendship to the uneducated, unskilled men who will come north looking to them as to a savior. Look what has happened in our own armies; our soldiers have been angered by the dark man who has assumed they were his friends. Sure, the North has talked loudly against slavery. I have joined in that talk, but I tell you, all of us are getting a little quieter when the question comes up as to what we are to do about the products of slavery."

Jethro tramped the frozen fields and thought of the things Ross Milton had said. He remembered the supper table that night in mid-April of 1861 and Wilse Graham's angry voice exclaiming, "Would yore abolitionists git the crocodile tears sloshed out of their eyes so they could take the black man by the hand? Would they say, 'We want you to come to our churches and yore children to come to our schools— why, we danged near fergit the difference in the colors of our skins because we air so almightly full of brotherly love!' Would it be like that in yore northern cities, Cousin John?"

The waiting for word of peace went on. February passed, the bitterest cold of the year coming as usual in that month. Then March came, breaking the back of winter with warmth permeating the cold, and with the smell of spring drifting daily to tease hope and to give shy promise of a coming radiance.

Then, finally, the fifth April of the war arrived, and in southern Illinois it came in a burst of warmth and color that seemed prophetic to those who waited for word from Washington. That fifth April had moved only into its second week when the news came that the guns were silent, that the terms of peace had been signed by two tired men somewhere in Virginia at a place called Appomattox Court House.

Jethro rode into Newton with Ed Turner and was allowed to spend the night with Ross Milton. By the time he reached the little county seat, the bunting was spread out by the yard, flags flew from almost every house, a long unused cannon boomed from the cliffs above the river. They had lifted the trapdoor in the roof of the jail, allowing the half-dozen delinquent citizens of the county to climb outside so their voices might add to the clamor. Men danced in the streets and embraced one another; some drank a continuous string of toasts to Lincoln, Grant, and a dozen others, until their bottles were empty and the compliments had to be started all over again with new purchases at one of the saloons. Others wept while they shouted; there was hardly a home in the county that had not felt the fiery lash of the war's tongue.

The editor took Jethro to the restaurant for supper. This time the place was milling with people who had come into town to celebrate. Plump Mrs. Hiles was bustling about in a near-frenzy, but she took time to speak to Jethro and to lament his golden curls, which had straightened out into a slightly waving thatch of light brown hair combed neatly back of the ears.

"You ain't as purty as you was three years ago, young Creighton," she said brightly. "You're gittin' a little of the owl-look of yore friend Red Milton here."

She clapped him on the back briefly and went on to her duties, knowing very well she had said a thing that pleased Matt Creighton's youngest boy.

That night there was a great display of fireworks, and then the town's band played while nearly a thousand voices joined in singing "The Battle Hymn of the Republic." Jethro's heart swelled in his breast. He thought suddenly of the tired face of the President.

"How I'd like to shake hands with him tonight," he thought. He turned to look at Ross Milton, who stood beside him, balanced painfully upon his crutches. The editor's eyes were fixed on something far away above the heads of the crowd, and Jethro noticed that tears were running down his cheeks.

At home the next day he tried to describe the details of the celebration to his parents and to Nancy, who listened with eyes as radiant as Jenny's used to be when she received her first letters from Shadrach. The little boys had caught some of their mother's happiness. "Do you remember him, Jeth?" they asked, with some awe of Jethro's thirteen years. "Do you remember what our pa looks like?"

Daily the color of April grew brighter. The apple and peach orchards were in bloom again, and the redbud was almost ready to burst. The little leaves on the silver poplars quivered in green and silver lights with every passing breeze, and Jenny's favorite lilacs bloomed in great thick clusters, deep purple and as fragrant as any beautiful thing on earth.

Then suddenly, because there were no longer any eyes to perceive it, the color was gone, and the fifth April had become, like her four older sisters, a time of grief and desolation.

People would ask for many years: "Where were you when you heard? What were you doing? Who brought you the word?"

Jethro would remember a sunlit field and a sense of serenity and happiness such as he had not known since early childhood. He would remember that he had stopped his team when he saw Nancy running toward him, that Nancy's face had been as white as it was during the days of waiting for a letter after the battle of Chickamauga, that she had sobbed against his shoulder.

He thought at first that something had happened to his father, or that word had come of John's being one of those last soldiers to die when peace was almost within reach.

Then Nancy said, "Jeth, it's the President—they've killed the President."

The work of the farm had to go on. Ellen had washed and scrubbed and cooked for her family the summer her three children had died, and in the spring of '65, Jethro went back to the fields and plowed the same furrows he had plowed for the past four years. But there was no longer any beauty in the world about him or any serenity in his heart. Sometimes he cried as the closing lines of his letter from the President flashed into his mind: "May God bless you for your earnest effort to seek out the right; may He guide both you and me in that search during the days to come." And again he remembered Ross Milton's words: "My hope lies in Abraham Lincoln. . . . if he can control the bigots, if he can allow the defeated their dignity—"

Little by little the story came through—details of the assassination, the attempted murder of the Secretary of State, the nation's wrath and woe. And then the news of a train on its way from the East, a train carrying Abraham Lincoln back to Springfield, Illinois.

One thought was with Jethro constantly during those April days as the train bearing the President made its slow journey across the miles toward Springfield.

"I want to see him; just once I want to look on his face. Springfield is only a hundred miles away. . . ."

But the hundred miles might just as well have been a thousand. The yoke of the farm had settled firmly across Jethro's shoulders; his work in the fields at the proper season was the sole source of food for his parents, for John's family, and for himself. There was no time or opportunity to go to Springfield, no hope of looking upon a face at once the plainest and the most beautiful, the humblest and the most magnificent, that Jethro would know in his lifetime.

It was the saddest and most cruel April of the five. It had held out an almost unbelievable joy and had then struck out in fury at those whose hands were outstretched. Jethro had learned to accept the whims of fate, schooled as he was in the philosophy of men who work the soil. The rains came or they were withheld, the heat ripened the grain or blasted it with a scorching flame, the ears of corn matured in golden beauty or they were infested by worms or blight. One accepted the good or the evil with humility, for life was a mystery, and questions were not for the lowly. But on the last Sunday of that April, a Sunday of sunlight and bright sky, Jethro lay in the grass on Walnut Hill, and rage mingled with the grief in his heart.

"Why did it happen? Why—why—did it have to happen?" He lay with his face close to the earth, clutching the fresh spring grass with both hands. "Never before has a president been killed; they've been looked after, watched over, and now this one, the one that has carried the load of this war till he's old and tired, the one that was my friend—"

He tried for a while to believe that the agony inside him was part of one of the nightmares that had recurred so often ever since the early stories of Wilson's Creek. But the warm April breeze stirred his hair, and the smell of the earth and the cry of the birds in the trees above him were a part of reality. This was no dream. Abraham Lincoln had been senselessly slain by the hand of a madman, and Jethro Creighton, with all the people of his time, had suffered an irreparable loss.

He heard steps approaching, and a moment later a hand was laid on his shoulder. He thought it might be Ed Turner or maybe old Israel Thomas, kind and full of sympathy, but of no help to him in this hour.

He could not talk, nor did he wish to listen, and so he lay quietly, hoping the intruder would go away and leave him to the pain of this latest and mightiest blow.

But the hand was not lifted, and after a long moment someone spoke. Recognition of the voice drew Jethro up in startled surprise. The man who knelt beside him was thin and gaunt, with a soft, dark beard covering his cheeks; he was a young man, but his eyes were tired, and there were a few strands of gray in his dark hair. Jethro would have passed him on the streets of Newton without recognizing him, but the voice had not changed. It was that of his teacher—his brother now—Shadrach Yale.

He had not embraced one of his brothers since the days of his very early childhood, but that morning he put his arms about Shadrach, and slowly the joy for the living assuaged a little the grief for the dead.

"Shad, it's a day I've dreamed about," he said, and even as he spoke, he vaguely wondered why it was that he should whisper the words.

Shadrach did not speak at first. He sat looking at Jethro as if he, in turn, doubted the reality of his senses. Finally he said, "Jeth—Jeth, how you have grown, how much you look like Bill—I can't believe it."

They were silent for a long time, each studying the other's face. An onlooker, not understanding the situation, would have wondered at the strange intensity of the two; an onlooker might have believed for a moment that they were man and boy suddenly bereft of their reason.

Jethro finally broke the silence. "Jenny?" he asked eagerly.

Shadrach smiled then. "She's up at the house, Jeth, all eagerness to see you. I asked if I might come out and find you first—it has been such a long time—"

"How did you get here, Shad? You didn't let us know."

"Mr. Milton met us in Olney last night and loaned us his horse and buggy to drive up here today. We wanted to surprise you; we had hoped it would be a perfect homecoming."

He paused, and Jethro understood. No perfect pearl. The editor had been right.

"I wanted to see him so much, Shad. Pa had said that maybe after the war was over I could go to Washington, maybe I could shake his hand."

Shadrach could only nod. He placed his hand for a second on Jethro's shoulder.

"Did you see him, Shad, more than the one time you wrote me about—the time he was ridin' with Grant?"

"We saw him that night, Jeth, the night of the fourteenth. Jenny and I had gone for a stroll after supper, and as we walked along we noticed that a little crowd had congregated, and then down the street we saw the President's carriage. There was some cheering, and he looked out at us and smiled. His face looked very old, but it was a happy face that night, I feel sure of that." Shadrach paused as if he were not sure he should say any more, but finally he continued. "We were awakened about eleven o'clock by noise and shouting in the street; we could understand only a few words of the shouting, but they were enough to make us dress and hurry outside. There was a soldier standing on the corner; he was crying, but he told us."

The distant horizon blurred a little, and the birds' trills and the soft golden blanket of sunlight over the fields and orchards seemed out of place—like laughter in a church.

Shadrach was speaking again. "I could take you to Springfield, Jeth. Mr. Milton and I talked about it last night; he doubts if it is best. There is no Abraham Lincoln for you to see, you know—only the empty shell. We think it would only hurt you."

"I reckon you're right."

"You're going to have help with the work this summer." Shadrach strove to bring lightness into his voice. "Jenny is going to help your mother; I'll go out to the fields with you. And John will be here in a few weeks. We saw him just a while before we left Washington."

Jethro nodded, while a crowd of thoughts raced through his mind. "Will you teach the school again next winter, Shad?"

Shadrach's eyes lighted at the question. "That is something I should let Jenny tell you, Jeth, but I can't. I'm going back to college. My uncle can get me a teaching position while I finish my work. And Jenny and I have decided that you're going with us. You've plowed long enough, Jeth; you're going to study now."

Jethro's hand found a sharp stick, and he dug it into the earth, twisted it around and around, and stared at the hole he had made as if it had some meaning.

"It would be the finest thing on earth for me, but what about my folks? My ma has lost three little boys and Mary—and Tom—and Bill. I'm the youngest; they depend on me."

"You are their pride, Jeth. Those two want the very best for you. And they won't be alone. Eb will be back, and there's always John. He wants you to get an education and then later to help his own boys along the same road. It's going to work out, Jeth; you'll see."

Jethro smiled slowly. "Don't build me up too much, Shad," he said after a while. "Somethin's like to break inside of me."

At that moment a voice sounded across the field from somewhere near the cabin. "Shad—Jeth—you two boys better come in now. I'm gettin' real vexed with both of you."

"Yes, let's go see Jenny," Jethro said huskily.

They walked together across the bridge that spanned Crooked Creek and through the half-acre south of the cabin, where four years before Jethro had helped his mother plant potatoes on a day when the news of Sumter had not quite reached the prairies.

A little distance up the road, past the hedge of lilacs and under the silver poplars of the dooryard, Jenny stood at the gate, waiting for them. She seemed taller in her city clothes, thinner and more delicate. But she was the same Jenny. Her arms were held out to Jethro, and for that moment when he ran toward her, all the shadows were lifted from the April morning.

RELATED READINGS

from The Boys' War
by Jim Murphy

A great number of Civil War soldiers on both sides were not much older than Jethro. In fact, an estimated 10 to 20 percent of the recruits were under the legal age of 18 when they signed up. This account tells what these young soldiers feared and why.

In order to be efficient fighters, boys in the Civil War had to put their normal fears and worries aside. This does not mean they lost all of their emotions. Far from it. These boys worried about a great deal— where their next meal would come from, the abilities and courage of the officers directly in charge of them, or how to get a good pair of shoes, to name just a few. But there were several specific concerns that were shared by all young soldiers on both sides.

One was a fear of being lost among the great crowds in which they marched and fought and died. It was not uncommon for an army of fifty or one hundred thousand men to look across a battlefield at an equal number of the enemy. This was nothing at all like home, where everybody knew the boys' names and faces. Here a boy was just another body, no more important than the person next to him. There are many accounts of boys, separated from their companies while either marching or fighting, who spent days and weeks trying to find a familiar face.

The biggest fear, however, was of being killed, and of not having their bodies identified properly. This was not as odd a fear as it might seem. After a major engagement, the battlefield would be a confusing, chaotic mess. The ground would be pockmarked with hundreds of craters, the result of the ceaseless cannon and mortar fire. Bits and pieces of shattered trees, cannons, and wagons would litter the earth, while the black smoke of burning buildings and fields created a murky and choking haze. Frightened and wounded horses galloped over the landscape; injured soldiers screamed for water or medical attention. A few wounded soldiers might be seen stumbling to find help, their shirts and pants saturated with blood, some still clinging to a severed arm.

What seeing such a scene must have felt like was captured by young Fred Grant, who had accompanied his father, Lieutenant General Ulysses S. Grant, during the siege of Vicksburg: "The horrors of a battlefield were brought vividly before me. I joined a detachment which was collecting the dead for burial. Sickening at the sights, I made my way with another detachment, which was gathering the wounded, to a log house which had been appropriated for a hospital. Here the scenes were so terrible that I became faint, and making my way to a tree, sat down, the most woebegone twelve-year-old in America."

The minute the shooting stopped, the men who had just fought in the battle went hunting among the churned-up landscape for their comrades, living and dead. Thomas Galway did this after the Battle of Gettysburg: "As for us, we have been attending our wounded and have been picking up such of our dead as we could recognize. Each regiment selects a suitable place for its dead and puts a head-board on each individual grave."

They attended to this chore with as much care as they could muster. They would, after all, want the same attention paid to their remains. But it must have been nearly impossible for the exhausted soldiers. For instance, when Grant's army drove toward Richmond in the spring of 1864, it suffered more than 61,000 casualties. Confederate records have not been preserved, but the South must have had similar losses. The dead who could not be identified, as well as all of the enemy dead, were consigned to a mass, unmarked grave, as Galway makes clear: "The unrecognized dead are left to the last, to be buried in long trenches. . . . The corpses are brought into rows and counted, the Confederate and Federals being separated into different rows. At the feet of each row of fifty or a hundred dead, a trench is dug about seven or eight feet wide and about three feet deep—for there is not time for a normal grave depth. Then the bodies, which are as black as ink and bloated from exposure to the sun, are placed in the shallow ditch and quickly covered with dirt."

Thousands of soldiers would die alone and be buried without proper religious services and in shallow graves. No one would ever know how they died and no one would ever be able to visit their place of burial. They would be lost forever. No wonder that Confederate soldier E. D. Patterson worried more about home than about the wounds he suffered: "I thought of home far away. . . . I wondered if my fate would ever be known to them. I had a horror of dying alone. . . . I was afraid that none of my regiment would ever find me, and that with the unknown dead who lay scattered around me I would be buried in one common ground. The thought was terrible. How I longed for day. Just that some one would see me die."

To die alone was something every young soldier feared. Yet those who managed to survive battle, but were taken prisoner or wounded, might have preferred that fate to the one that awaited them. For if aspects of the fighting represented a shift to modern warfare, the treatment of prisoners and the sick and wounded was something directly out of the Dark Ages.

While anger and embarrassment at being captured may have helped these boys add drama to their accounts, their suffering was real. "Colonel Davis calls it the Black Hole of Calcutta," John Delhaney said of Fort Henry, the prison he was taken to after being captured at Gettysburg. "Our settling down consists in spreading our blankets on the filthy floor, and although many of us are wounded severely enough to merit beds, but one or two are given even bunks, and these are glad enough to leave them to their former occupants—the vermin."

Supplies of all kinds were lacking, and many boys report having to get their blankets and clothes from the bodies of dead men. Food, always a concern of the soldier, was in even shorter supply. Union soldiers voiced the same complaints about their prison conditions. One boy managed to scratch out a fast description of one of his meals: "Rations at last; one course meal cracker and a small bit of bacon: one ration. We are informed that these rations were issued in advance for the following twenty-four hours. Useless to protest; we had but one remaining right—the right to submit. 'That's the best we can do; we are short of rations for our own troops,' said the major. Most of us devoured the 'twenty-four hours rations in advance' at one standing."

These wretched conditions were made even more horrid by overcrowding. The worst Union prison camp was in Elmira New York, and contained ninety-six hundred prisoners inside a forty-acre enclosure. The Southern prison at Andersonville, Georgia, is considered the most fiendish. It was a sixteen-acre stockade camp designed to hold ten thousand prisoners. But by August of 1864, more than thirty-three thousand had been crammed within its walls without any shelter from the hot summer sun.

A Confederate boy visited the Andersonville prison and came away with these thoughts: "The prison struck me as being at best but a miserable makeshift. The day I saw them they were a sweltering mass of humanity, each unit of which was confined to a space of not more than twenty feet. This of itself—the crowding of thirty-two thousand human beings so thickly together—was sufficient to make the prison unsanitary. But that was not all. I saw whole carcasses of slaughtered animals being cut up and made ready for distribution. The refuse which fell into the creek, together with the filth that washed into it from the hillside during heavy rains, necessarily contaminated the water. . . . I venture to say that on the day I was at Andersonville fully a thousand were in the hospital, and that nearly as many more were sick in the stockade. . . . I don't know exactly how many died that day, but in all probability a hundred at least; for according to the hospital records, the average daily death rate for the month of August, 1864, was fully that number."

The conditions at Andersonville were so bad that it became a death camp. Of the forty-five thousand Union soldiers who were imprisoned there, over thirteen thousand would die of sickness, malnutrition, or exposure. After the war, the commandant of Andersonville, Henry Wirz, would be tried and executed for war crimes—the only such trial to result from the Civil War.

How did these boys manage to survive the ordeal of imprisonment? No doubt their strong, young bodies helped them endure the heat or cold. Many used their imaginations and skills. After telling about the lack of food and water at his prison, Point Lookout in Maryland, one Southern boy noted: "The prisoners carried on all kinds of business. Some made finger rings and breastpins out of gutta purcha [a rubberlike substance made from tree sap], toothpicks and trinkets of different kinds of old bones. I myself was engaged in making crude jewelry, from the proceeds of which I was enabled to purchase many luxuries, such as corn meal, coffee, sugar and tobacco. We found ready sale for such stuff, principally among sympathizers on the outside."

Many took a more direct approach to getting more food, as this Union boy's diary entry makes clear: "Sept. 13th, 1863. Rats are found to be very good for food, and every night many are captured and slain. So pressing is the want of food that nearly all who can have gone into the rat business, either selling these horrid animals or killing them and eating them. There are numbers in the drains and under the houses and they are so tame that they hardly think it worth while to get out of our way when we meet them."

No doubt most of a prisoner's time was spent searching for food and clean water, or trying to make himself comfortable. Despite these struggles, many tell of evenings filled with the singing of popular songs or religious hymns. "Another source of recreation," one boy mentions, "is a quiet promenade during the cool hours of evening. Then you may see hundreds of promenaders passing up and down the prison enclosure in quiet, pleasant, but melancholy converse."

Activity in prison was low-key and energy-saving. But John Delhaney did note one intriguing game that seemed to have captured the fancy of many of his fellow prisoners: "The prisoners nearly every evening are engaged in a game they call 'base-ball,' which notwithstanding the heat they prosecute with persevering energy. I don't understand the game, as there is a great deal of running and little apparent gain, but those who play it get very excited over it, and it appears to be fine exercise."

While life in prison must have seemed like a living hell to those who were captured, the worst fate was for the wounded and sick. The weapons used in the Civil War had ten times the killing power of those used in the Revolutionary War. Flesh was ripped and eyes punctured by flying pieces of metal, cannon shells severed arms and legs with ease, and, because metal helmets were not yet worn, head injuries were very common. Unfortunately, the doctor's ability to treat these wounds or simply to lessen pain was primitive at best.

The science of doctoring was still in its infancy when the Civil War started. Morphine and chloroform were used to ease pain, and when these ran short, whiskey and bourbon had to do. Iron pokers were heated until they were white-hot and then applied directly to wounds to stop the bleeding. And if a wound to an arm or leg seemed too severe or became infected, the usual course of action was to cut off the limb.

After one battle, Elisha Stockwell came upon this scene: "We moved on to the east side of town where they were fetching the wounded. They were laying them in rows with just room to walk between. They had tents for those that were the worst off, and where they were amputating arms and legs. There was a wash-out back of one tent that had a wagon load of arms and legs. The legs had the shoes and stockings on them."

Even minor wounds might end up with what we might consider very drastic treatment. While imprisoned, John Delhaney happened to meet a Union army surgeon: "He is a very fine looking man and has his hand in a sling, for yesterday when operating upon a gangrened wound, the knife with which he was operating cut his finger slightly; and [fearing infection] he very sensibly had his own finger immediately amputated."

Most soldiers looked upon the doctor's work as useless mutilation heaped on top of injury, and the fact that large numbers of the injured would linger in agonizing pain for days only to die did not enhance the reputation of the medical profession. One boy, obviously very angry, wrote a blunt condemnation of what he was witnessing: "I believe the Doctors kills more than they cour. Doctors haint Got half Sence."

Unless absolutely necessary, most soldiers would stay as far away from the doctors as possible and treat themselves as best as they could. Teas made from the bark of slippery elm, willow, and dogwood trees were favored remedies for anything from a cold to infected wounds. Wounds were treated by daily cleaning and the removal of anything foreign.

"Today," wrote a young soldier with several wounds to his leg and back, "Sheppard who is most kind in his attentions to my wounds extracts therefrom 4 maggots and cleanses the wounds thoroughly. They are doing very well now; I mean my wounds." One week later he writes, "Sheppard extracts from my wound several pieces of my pantaloons that had been carried into my leg by the bullet and which worked themselves back to the surface today, taking twenty-two days to go a distance of about 2 inches." All of this was done without any sort of painkiller or antiseptic. Surprisingly, this boy recovered from his wounds.

While bullets and shells accounted for tens of thousands of injuries, more Civil War soldiers were felled by sickness and disease. The sanitary conditions of the camps and prisons were deplorable; drinking water and food were often contaminated. In addition, this was the first time these men had lived in such large groups, which facilitated the spread of fever. Dysentery and diarrhea were the most common diseases. But malaria, pneumonia, bronchitis, and scurvy were also common.

Oddly, measles, a disease we consider relatively harmless, turned out to be a major problem for boys in the Civil War. Once the disease took hold, it could sweep through a camp in a matter of days. One gathering of ten thousand new recruits was hit by measles, and before the week was out, more than four thousand had contracted the disease. The disease was so common that it became standard procedure to withhold new troops from active duty until they were "put through the measles."

The treatment for all of these diseases was bed rest and plenty of liquids. Even so, one statistician estimates that more than half of all the deaths in the Civil War were caused by fevers! A boy, J. W. Love, may have summed up the situation perfectly in his letter home: "T. G. Freman is Ded and they is Several mor that is Dangerous with the fever. They hev been 11 Died with the fever in Co. A since we left hinston and 2 died that was wounded so you now See that these Big Battles is not as Bad as the fever."

The Mysterious Mr. Lincoln

by Russell Freedman

Across Five Aprils *makes it clear that people had very mixed feelings about their President, Abraham Lincoln. Unlike Jethro, many thought he was the worst possible person for the job. This selection from* Lincoln, A Photobiography, *can help you understand why people judged Lincoln so differently.*

"If any personal description of me is thought desirable, it may be said, I am, in height, six feet, four inches, nearly; lean in flesh, weighing, on average, one hundred and eighty pounds; dark complexion, with coarse black hair and grey eyes— no other marks or brands recollected."

Abraham Lincoln wasn't the sort of man who could lose himself in a crowd. After all, he stood six feet four inches tall, and to top it off, he wore a high silk hat.

His height was mostly in his long bony legs. When he sat in a chair, he seemed no taller than anyone else. It was only when he stood up that he towered above other men.

At first glance, most people thought he was homely. Lincoln thought so too, referring once to his "poor, lean, lank face." As a young man he was sensitive about his gawky looks, but in time, he learned to laugh at himself. When a rival called him "two-faced" during a political debate, Lincoln replied: "I leave it to my audience. If I had another face, do you think I'd wear this one?"

According to those who knew him, Lincoln was a man of many faces. In repose, he often seemed sad and gloomy. But when he began to speak, his expression changed. "The dull, listless features dropped like a mask," said a Chicago newspaperman. "The eyes began to sparkle, the mouth to smile, the whole countenance was wreathed in animation, so that a stranger would have said, 'Why, this man, so angular and solemn a moment ago, is really handsome!'"

Lincoln was the most photographed man of his time, but his friends insisted that no photo ever did him justice. It's no wonder. Back then, cameras required long exposures. The person being photographed had to "freeze" as the seconds ticked by. If he blinked an eye, the picture would be blurred. That's why Lincoln looks so stiff and formal in his photos. We never see him laughing or joking.

And it's true that he carried his folksy manners and homespun speech to the White House with him. He said "howdy" to visitors and invited them to "stay a spell." He greeted diplomats while wearing carpet slippers, called his wife "mother" at receptions, and told bawdy jokes at cabinet meetings.

Lincoln may have seemed like a common man, but he wasn't. His friends agreed that he was one of the most ambitious people they had ever known. Lincoln struggled hard to rise above his log-cabin origins, and he was proud of his achievements. By the time he ran for president he was a wealthy man, earning a large income from his law practice and his many investments. As for the nickname Abe, he hated it. No one who knew him well ever called him Abe to his face. They addressed him as Lincoln or Mr. Lincoln.

Lincoln is often described as a sloppy dresser, careless about his appearance. In fact, he patronized the best tailor in Springfield, Illinois, buying two suits a year. That was at a time when many men lived, died, and were buried in the same suit.

It's true that Lincoln had little formal "eddication," as he would have pronounced it. Almost everything he "larned" he taught himself. All his life he said "thar" for *there,* "git" for *get,* "kin" for *can.* Even so, he became an eloquent public speaker who could hold a vast audience spellbound, and a great writer whose finest phrases still ring in our ears. He was known to sit up late into the night, discussing Shakespeare's plays with White House visitors.

He was certainly a humorous man, famous for his rollicking stories. But he was also moody and melancholy, tormented by long and frequent bouts of depression. Humor was his therapy. He relied on his yarns, a friend observed, to "whistle down sadness."

He had a cool, logical mind, trained in the courtroom, and a practical, commonsense approach to problems. Yet he was deeply superstitious, a believer in dreams, omens, and visions.

Artists and writers tried to capture the "real" Lincoln that the camera missed, but something about the man always escaped them. His changeable features, his tones, gestures, and expressions, seemed to defy description.

Today it's hard to imagine Lincoln as he really was. And he never cared to reveal much about himself. In company he was witty and talkative, but he rarely betrayed his inner feelings. According to William Herndon, his law partner, he was "the most secretive—reticent—shut-mouthed man that ever lived."

In his own time, Lincoln was never fully understood even by his closest friends. Since then, his life story has been told and retold so many times, he has become as much a legend as a flesh-and-blood human being. While the legend is based on truth, it is only partly true. And it hides the man behind it like a disguise.

The legendary Lincoln is known as Honest Abe, a humble man of the people who rose from a log cabin to the White House. There's no doubt that Lincoln was a poor boy who made good.

We admire Lincoln today as an American folk hero. During the Civil War, however, he was the most unpopular president the nation had ever known. His critics called him a tyrant, a hick, a stupid baboon who was unfit for his office. As commander in chief of the armed forces, he was denounced as a bungling amateur who meddled in military affairs he knew nothing about. But he also had his supporters. They praised him as a farsighted statesman, a military mastermind who engineered the Union victory.

Lincoln is best known as the Great Emancipator, the man who freed the slaves. Yet he did not enter the war with that idea in mind. "My paramount object in this struggle *is* to save the Union," he said in 1862, "and is *not* either to save or destroy slavery." As the war continued, Lincoln's attitude changed. Eventually he came to regard the conflict as a moral crusade to wipe out the sin of slavery.

No black leader was more critical of Lincoln than the fiery abolitionist writer and editor Frederick Douglass. Douglass had grown up as a slave. He had won his freedom by escaping to the North. Early in the war, impatient with Lincoln's cautious leadership, Douglass called him "preeminently the white man's president, entirely devoted to the welfare of white men." Later, Douglass changed his mind and came to admire Lincoln. Several years after the war, he said this about the sixteenth president:

"His greatest mission was to accomplish two things: first, to save his country from dismemberment and ruin; and, second, to free his country from the great crime of slavery. . . . taking him for all in all, measuring the tremendous magnitude of the work before him, considering the necessary means to ends, and surveying the end from the beginning, infinite wisdom has seldom sent any man into the world better fitted for his mission than Abraham Lincoln."

The Gettysburg Address

by Abraham Lincoln

When he read the newspaper, Jethro was unsure as to whether Lincoln's speech at Gettysburg was "a great one or just another speech." His mother said of the speech, "It has the ring of Scriptures about it." Read it through carefully to decide how you feel.

Fourscore and seven years ago, our fathers brought forth on this continent a new nation, conceived in Liberty and dedicated to the proposition that all men are created equal.

Now we are engaged in a great civil war, testing whether that nation, or any nation so conceived and so dedicated, can long endure. We are met on a great battlefield of that war. We have come to dedicate a portion of that field, as a final resting place for those who here gave their lives that that nation might live. It is altogether fitting and proper that we should do this.

But, in a larger sense, we can not dedicate—we can not consecrate—we can not hallow—this ground. The brave men, living and dead, who struggled here have consecrated it far above our poor power to add or detract. The world will little note nor long remember what we say here, but it can never forget what they did here. It is for us the living, rather, to be dedicated here to the unfinished work which they who fought here have thus far so nobly advanced. It is rather for us to be here dedicated to the great task remaining before us—that from these honored dead we take increased devotion to that cause for which they gave the last full measure of devotion—that we here highly resolve that these dead shall not have died in vain—that this nation, under God, shall have a new birth of freedom—and that government of the people, by the people, for the people, shall not perish from the earth.

The Drummer Boy of Shiloh

by Ray Bradbury

In this story, Ray Bradbury imagines what might have been going through the minds of an important general and one of the youngest in his command on the night of April 5, 1862, just hours before one of the bloodiest battles of the Civil War. How different do you think their conversation would have been if the general and the drummer boy had met two nights later, after more than 10,000 Union soldiers, including 19-year-old Tom Creighton, had died at Shiloh?

In the April night, more than once, blossoms fell from the orchard trees and lit with rustling taps on the drumskin. At midnight a peach stone left miraculously on a branch through winter, flicked by a bird, fell swift and unseen, struck once, like panic, which jerked the boy upright. In silence he listened to his own heart ruffle away, away, at last gone from his ears and back in his chest again.

After that, he turned the drum on its side, where its great lunar face peered at him whenever he opened his eyes.

His face, alert or at rest, was solemn. It was indeed a solemn time and a solemn night for a boy just turned fourteen in the peach field near the Owl Creek not far from the church at Shiloh.

". . . thirty-one, thirty-two, thirty-three . . ."

Unable to see, he stopped counting.

Beyond the thirty-three familiar shadows, forty

thousand men, exhausted by nervous expectation, unable to sleep for romantic dreams of battles yet unfought, lay crazily askew in their uniforms. A mile yet farther on, another army was strewn helter-skelter, turning slow, basting themselves with the thought of what they would do when the time came: a leap, a yell, a blind plunge their strategy, raw youth their protection and benediction.

Now and again the boy heard a vast wind come up, that gently stirred the air. But he knew what it was, the army here, the army there, whispering to itself in the dark. Some men talking to others, others murmuring to themselves, and all so quiet it was like a natural element arisen from south or north with the motion of the earth toward dawn.

What the men whispered the boy could only guess, and he guessed that it was: Me, I'm the one, I'm the one of all the rest won't die. I'll live through it. I'll go home. The band will play. And I'll be there to hear it.

Yes, thought the boy, that's all very well for them, they can give as good as they get!

For with the careless bones of the young men harvested by night and bundled around campfires were the similarly strewn steel bones of their rifles, with bayonets fixed like eternal lightning lost in the orchard grass.

Me, thought the boy, I got only a drum, two sticks to beat it, and no shield.

There wasn't a man-boy on this ground tonight did not have a shield he cast, riveted or carved himself on his way to his first attack, compounded of remote but nonetheless firm and fiery family devotion, flag-blown patriotism and cocksure immortality strengthened by the touchstone of very real gunpowder, ramrod, minnieball and flint. But without these last the boy felt his family move yet farther off away in the dark, as if one of those great prairie-burning trains had chanted them away never to return, leaving him with this drum which was worse than a toy in the game to be played tomorrow or some day much too soon.

The boy turned on his side. A moth brushed his face, but it was peach blossom. A peach blossom flicked him, but it was a moth. Nothing stayed put. Nothing had a name. Nothing was as it once was.

If he lay very still, when the dawn came up and the soldiers put on their bravery with their caps, perhaps they might go away, the war with them, and not notice him lying small here, no more than a toy himself.

"Well, by God, now," said a voice.

The boy shut up his eyes, to hide inside himself, but it was too late. Someone, walking by in the night, stood over him.

"Well," said the voice quietly, "here's a soldier crying *before* the fight. Good. Get it over. Won't be time once it all starts."

And the voice was about to move on when the boy, startled, touched the drum at his elbow. The man above, hearing this, stopped. The boy could feel his eyes, sense him slowly bending near. A hand must have come down out of the night, for there was a little rat-tat as the fingernails brushed and the man's breath fanned his face.

"Why, it's the drummer boy, isn't it?"

The boy nodded, not knowing if his nod was seen. "Sir, is that *you?*" he said.

"I assume it is." The man's knees cracked as he bent still closer.

He smelled as all fathers should smell, of salt sweat, ginger tobacco, horse and boot leather, and the earth he walked upon. He had many eyes. No, not eyes, brass buttons that watched the boy.

He could only be, and was, the General.

"What's your name, boy?" he asked.

"Joby," whispered the boy, starting to sit up.

"All right, Joby, don't stir." A hand pressed his chest gently, and the boy relaxed. "How long you been with us, Joby?"

"Three weeks, sir."

"Run off from home or joined legitimately, boy?"

Silence.

"Damn-fool question," said the General. "Do you shave yet, boy? Even more of a damn-fool. There's your cheek, fell right off the tree overhead. And the others here not much older. Raw, raw, damn raw, the lot of you. You ready for tomorrow or the next day, Joby?"

"I think so, sir."

"You want to cry some more, go on ahead. I did the same last night."

"*You,* sir?"

"God's truth. Thinking of everything ahead. Both sides figuring the other side will just give up, and soon, and the war done in weeks, and us all home. Well, that's not how it's going to be. And maybe that's why I cried."

"Yes, sir," said Joby.

The General must have taken out a cigar now, for the dark was suddenly filled with the Indian smell of tobacco unlit as yet, but chewed as the man thought what next to say.

"It's going to be a crazy time," said the General. "Counting both sides, there's a hundred thousand men, give or take a few thousand out there tonight, not one as can spit a sparrow off a tree, or knows a horse clod from a minnieball. Stand up, bare the breast, ask to be a target, thank them and sit down, that's us, that's them. We should turn tail and train four months, they should do the same. But here we are, taken with spring fever and thinking it blood lust, taking our sulphur with cannons instead of with molasses as it should be, going to be a hero, going to live forever. And I can see all of them over there nodding agreement, save the other way around. It's wrong, boy, it's wrong as a head put on hind side front and a man marching backward through life. It will be a double massacre if one of their itchy generals decides to picnic his lads on our grass. More innocents will get shot out of pure Cherokee enthusiasm than ever got shot before. Owl Creek was full of boys splashing around in the noonday sun just a few hours ago. I fear it will be full of boys again, just floating, at sundown tomorrow, not caring where the tide takes them."

The General stopped and made a little pile of winter leaves and twigs in the darkness, as if he might at any moment strike fire to them to see his way through the coming days when the sun might not show its face because of what was happening here and just beyond.

The boy watched the hand stirring the leaves and opened his lips to say something, but did not say it. The General heard the boy's breath and spoke himself.

"Why am I telling you this? That's what you wanted to ask, eh? Well, when you got a bunch of wild horses on a loose rein somewhere, somehow you got to bring order, rein them in. These lads, fresh out of the milkshed, don't know what I know, and I can't tell them: men actually die, in war. So each is his own army. I got to make *one* army of them. And for that, boy, I need you."

"Me!" The boy's lips barely twitched.

"Now, boy," said the General quietly, "you are the heart of the army. Think of that. You're the heart of the army. Listen, now."

And, lying there, Joby listened.

And the General spoke on.

If he, Joby, beat slow tomorrow, the heart would beat slow in the men. They would lag by the wayside. They would drowse in the fields on their muskets. They would sleep forever, after that, in those same fields, their hearts slowed by a drummer boy and stopped by enemy lead.

But if he beat a sure, steady, ever faster rhythm, then, then their knees would come up in a long line down over that hill, one knee after the other, like a wave on the ocean shore! Had he seen the ocean ever? Seen the waves rolling in like a well-ordered cavalry charge to the sand? Well, that was it, that's what he wanted, that's what was needed! Joby was his right hand and his left. He gave the orders, but Joby set the pace!

So bring the right knee up and the right foot out and the left knee up and the left foot out. One following the other in good time, in brisk time. Move the blood up the body and make the head proud and the spine stiff and the jaw resolute. Focus the eye and set the teeth, flare the nostrils and tighten the hands, put steel armor all over the men, for blood moving fast in them does indeed make men feel as if they'd put on steel. He must keep at it, at it! Long and steady, steady and long! Then, even though shot or torn, those wounds got in hot blood—in blood he'd helped stir— would feel less pain. If their blood was cold, it would be more than slaughter, it would be murderous nightmare and pain best not told and no one to guess.

The General spoke and stopped, letting his breath slack off. Then, after a moment, he said, "So there you are, that's it. Will you do that, boy? Do you know now you're general of the army when the General's left behind?"

The boy nodded mutely.

"You'll run them through for me then, boy?"

"Yes, sir."

"Good. And, God willing, many nights from tonight, many years from now, when you're as old or far much older than me, when they ask you what you did in this awful time, you will tell them—one part humble and one part proud—'I was the drummer boy at the battle of Owl Creek,' or the Tennessee River, or maybe they'll just name it after the church there. 'I was the drummer boy at Shiloh.' Good grief, that has a beat and sound to it fitting for Mr. Longfellow. 'I was the drummer boy at Shiloh.' Who will ever hear those words and not know you, boy, or what you thought this night, or what you'll think tomorrow or the next day when we must get up on our legs and *move!*"

The general stood up. "Well, then. God bless you, boy. Good night."

"Good night, sir."

And, tobacco, brass, boot polish, salt sweat and leather, the man moved away through the grass.

Joby lay for a moment, staring but unable to see where the man had gone.

He swallowed. He wiped his eyes. He cleared his throat. He settled himself. Then, at last, very slowly and firmly, he turned the drum so that it faced up toward the sky.

He lay next to it, his arm around it, feeling the tremor, the touch, the muted thunder as, all the rest of the April night in the year 1862, near the Tennessee River, not far from the Owl Creek, very close to the church named Shiloh, the peach blossoms fell on the drum.

Around the Campfire

by Andrew Hudgins

*This poem could be a memory from
almost any battlefield campground during
the Civil War.*

Around the campfire we sang hymns.
When asked I'd play my flute, and lay
a melody between night's
incessant cannonfire that boomed
5   irregularly, but with the depth
of kettle drums. Occasionally,
in lulls, we'd hear a fading snatch
of Yankee song sucked to us in
the backwash of their cannonballs.
10   These are, oddly enough, fond memories.

One night, a Texas boy sat down
and strummed a homemade banjo.
He'd bought it for a canteen full
of corn. He followed me around
15   and pestered me to teach him notes.
He loved that ragged box but, Lord,
he couldn't play it worth a damn.
Nobody could. I tried to tell him so.
"Hell, I know, Sid," he said. "If I
20   were any good, I would worry me
too much. This way I can just blame
the instrument."
                  And this, too, is
a fond instructive memory.

25   *Boom BOOM.* "Listen to *that,*" he said.
Then silence once again as Yanks
swabbed out the cannonbarrel and rammed
another charge into the gun. They paused
a minute in their work. *Boom BOOM.*
30   Our cannon fired in answer to
in-coming shells. "Don't they," he asked
"sound like a giant limping through
the woods in search of us?" I laughed.
It was a peaceful night and we
35   were working on some liquid corn.
Boom BOOM. I filled my cup again
and said, "He's after us all right."
He laughed. *Boom BOOM.* I sloshed more in
his cup. A shell exploded to our right.
40   A piece of shrapnel nicked my ear,
and when the smoke had cleared, I saw
him sitting, looking for his cup
and for the hand he'd held it in.

From this, I didn't learn a thing.

The Huts at Esquimaux

by Norman Dubie

John's letter to Nancy tells about the terrible struggle that took place around Chattanooga between September and November of 1863. Although written in the 1980s, this poem reads like a letter from another soldier at the same battle.

For Dave Smith

Our clothes are still wet from wading
The Chickamauga last evening.
There is heavy frost. We have
Walked on the dead all night.
5   Now in the firelight
We are exchanging shells and grape shot.

I can still hear our loud huzza
When late in the day
The enemy fell into full retreat
10   Along the pine ridge to the East . . .

We chased them until we were weary.
Each night this week
There's been something
To keep me from sleep. Just an hour ago
15   I saw

A dead sharp-shooter sitting
Against a rock with a scallop
Of biscuit still lodged in his mouth.

He wore one silk sock.

20   Snediker has returned from Chattanooga
        With five thousand convalescents
        For the left wing of their musketry.

        We have roasted a deer
        With a molasses sauce and pepper.
25   Magrill and Zandt have returned
        From horse hunting with a sack of sugar.
        By morning we will have buried our dead
        And fed the prisoners: Joe Cotton

        Will hang all seven of them in one tree
30   When he sees they're done
        Licking their fingers . . .

        I shot a Rebel yesterday
        In high water just for cursing me.
        Just six months ago
35   For that alone it would have meant
        Three days in stockade.

        We can see now that cannonading
        Has set the hillside on fire.
        The wounded Grays
40   Will be burned
        Beyond their Christian names . . .

        Joe Cotton says he'd ask God
        For rain, but he's got no tent
        And river water
45   Has chilled him straight through

        To the very quick of his being.

The Sniper

by Liam O'Flaherty

The American Civil War is by no means the only conflict to pit family and friends against each other. "The Sniper" is set in Ireland between 1917 and 1919, when the Irish were fighting both for and against independence from England. Sadly, the sniper in this story might be found on the rooftops of cities all over the world today.

The long June twilight faded into night. Dublin lay enveloped in darkness, but for the dim light of the moon, that shone through fleecy clouds, casting a pale light as of approaching dawn over the streets and the dark waters of the Liffey. Around the beleaguered Four Courts the heavy guns roared. Here and there through the city machine guns and rifles broke the silence of the night, spasmodically, like dogs barking on lone farms. Republicans and Free Staters were waging civil war.

On a roof-top near O'Connel Bridge, a Republican sniper lay watching. Beside him lay his rifle and over his shoulders were slung a pair of field-glasses. His face was the face of a student—thin and ascetic, but his eyes had the cold gleam of the fanatic. They were deep and thoughtful, the eyes of a man, who is used to look at death.

He was eating a sandwich hungrily. He had eaten nothing since morning. He had been too excited to eat. He finished the sandwich, and taking a flask of whiskey from his pocket, he took a short draught. Then he returned the flask to his pocket. He paused for a moment, considering whether he should risk a smoke. It was dangerous. The flash might be seen in the darkness and there were enemies watching. He decided to take the risk. Placing a cigarette between his lips, he struck a match, inhaled the smoke hurriedly and put out the light. Almost immediately, a bullet flattened itself against the parapet of the roof. The sniper took another whiff and put out the cigarette. Then he swore softly and crawled away to the left.

Cautiously he raised himself and peered over the parapet. There was a flash and a bullet whizzed over his head. He dropped immediately. He had seen the flash. It came from the opposite side of the street.

He rolled over the roof to a chimney stack in the rear, and slowly drew himself up behind it, until his eyes were level with the top of the parapet. There was nothing to be seen—just the dim outline of the opposite housetop against the blue sky. His enemy was under cover.

Just then an armoured car came across the bridge and advanced slowly up the street. It stopped on the opposite side of the street fifty yards ahead. The sniper could hear the dull panting of the motor. His heart beat faster. It was an enemy car. He wanted to fire, but he knew it was useless. His bullets would never pierce the steel that covered the grey monster.

Then round the corner of a side street came an old woman, her head covered by a tattered shawl. She began to talk to the man in the turret of the car. She was pointing to the roof where the sniper lay. An informer.

The turret opened. A man's head and shoulders appeared, looking towards the sniper. The sniper raised his rifle and fired. The head fell heavily on the turret wall. The woman darted toward the side street. The sniper fired again. The woman whirled round and fell with a shriek into the gutter.

Suddenly from the opposite roof a shot rang out and the sniper dropped his rifle with a curse. The rifle clattered to the roof. The sniper thought the noise would wake the dead. He stopped to pick the rifle up. He couldn't lift it. His fore-arm was dead. "Christ," he muttered, "I'm hit."

Dropping flat on to the roof, he crawled back to the parapet. With his left hand he felt the injured right fore-arm. The blood was oozing through the sleeve of his coat. There was no pain—just a deadened sensation, as if the arm had been cut off.

Quickly he drew his knife from his pocket, opened it on the breastwork of the parapet and ripped open the sleeve. There was a small hole where the bullet had entered. On the other side there was no hole. The bullet had lodged in the bone. It must have fractured it. He bent the arm below the wound. The arm bent back easily. He ground his teeth to overcome the pain.

Then, taking out his field dressing, he ripped open the packet with his knife. He broke the neck of the iodine bottle and let the bitter fluid drip into the wound. A paroxysm of pain swept through him. He placed the cotton wadding over the wound and wrapped the dressing over it. He tied the end with his teeth.

Then he lay still against the parapet, and closing his eyes, he made an effort of will to overcome the pain.

In the street beneath all was still. The armoured car had retired speedily over the bridge, with the machine gunner's head hanging lifeless over the turret. The woman's corpse lay still in the gutter.

The sniper lay for a long time nursing his wounded arm and planning escape. Morning must not find him wounded on the roof. The enemy on the opposite roof covered his escape. He must kill that enemy and he could not use his rifle. He had only a revolver to do it. Then he thought of a plan.

Taking off his cap, he placed it over the muzzle of his rifle. Then he pushed the rifle slowly upwards over the parapet, until the cap was visible from the opposite side of the street. Almost immediately there was a report, and a bullet pierced the centre of the cap. The sniper slanted the rifle forward. The cap slipped down into the street. Then, catching the rifle in the middle, the sniper dropped his left hand over the roof and let it hang, lifelessly. After a few moments he let the rifle drop to the street. Then he sank to the roof, dragging his hand with him.

Crawling quickly to the left, he peered up at the corner of the roof. His ruse had succeeded. The other sniper, seeing the cap and rifle fall, thought that he had killed his man. He was now standing before a row of chimney pots, looking across, with his head clearly silhouetted against the western sky.

The Republican sniper smiled and lifted his revolver above the edge of the parapet. The distance was about fifty yards—a hard shot in the dim light, and his right arm was paining him like a thousand devils. He took a steady aim. His hand trembled with eagerness. Pressing his lips together, he took a deep breath through his nostrils and fired. He was almost deafened with the report and his arm shook with the recoil.

Then, when the smoke cleared, he peered across and uttered a cry of joy. His enemy had been hit. He was reeling over the parapet in his death agony. He struggled to keep his feet, but he was slowly falling forward, as if in a dream. The rifle fell from his grasp, hit the parapet, fell over, bounded off the pole of a barber's shop beneath and then cluttered on to the pavement.

Then the dying man on the roof crumpled up and fell forward. The body turned over and over in space and hit the ground with a dull thud. Then it lay still.

The sniper looked at his enemy falling and he shuddered. The lust of battle died in him. He became bitten by remorse. The sweat stood out in beads on his forehead. Weakened by his wound and the long summer day of fasting and watching on the roof, he revolted from the sight of the shattered mass of his dead enemy. His teeth chattered. He began to gibber to himself, cursing the war, cursing himself, cursing everybody.

He looked at the smoking revolver in his hand and with an oath he hurled it to the roof at his feet. The revolver went off with the concussion, and the bullet whizzed past the sniper's head. He was frightened back to his senses by the shock. His nerves steadied. The cloud of fear scattered from his mind and he laughed.

Taking the whiskey flask from his pocket, he emptied it at a draught. He felt reckless under the influence of the spirits. He decided to leave the roof and look for his company commander to report. Everywhere around was quiet. There was not much danger in going through the streets. He picked up his revolver and put it in his pocket. Then he crawled down through the sky-light to the house underneath.

When the sniper reached the laneway on the street level, he felt a sudden curiosity as to the identity of the enemy sniper whom he had killed. He decided that he was a good shot whoever he was. He wondered if he knew him. Perhaps he had been in his own company before the split in the army. He decided to risk going over to have a look at him. He peered around the corner into O'Connell Street. In the upper part of the street there was heavy firing, but around here all was quiet.

The sniper darted across the street. A machine gun tore up the ground around him with a hail of bullets, but he escaped. He threw himself face downwards beside the corpse. The machine gun stopped.

Then the sniper turned over the dead body and looked into his brother's face.

from Voices from the Battlefield

by Milton Meltzer

These three letters from Civil War soldiers show several reasons why soldiers deserted. They also suggest different points of view about how and why deserters should be punished.

As the range grew better, the firing became more rapid, the situation desperate and exasperating to the last degree. Human nature was on the rack, and there burst forth from it the most vehement, terrible swearing I have ever heard. Certainly the joy of conflict was not ours that day. The suspense was only for a moment, however, for the order to charge came just after. Whether the regiment was thrown into disorder or not, I never knew. I only remember that as we rose and started, all the fire that had been held back so long was loosed. In a second the air was full of the hiss of bullets and the hurtle of grapeshot. . . . I see again, as I saw it then in a flash, a man just in front of me drop his musket and throw up his hands, stung into vigorous swearing by a bullet behind the ear. Many men fell going up the hill, but it seemed to be all over in a moment, and I found myself passing a hollow where a dozen wounded men lay—among them our sergeant-major, who was calling me to come down. He had caught sight of the blanket rolled across my back, and called me to unroll it and help to carry from the field one of our wounded lieutenants.

When I returned from obeying this summons the

regiment was not to be seen. It had gone in on the run, what there was left of it, and had disappeared in the cornfield about the battery. There was nothing to do but lie there and await developments. Nearly all the men in the hollow were wounded, one man frightfully so, his arm being cut short off. He lived a few minutes only. All were calling for water, of course, but none was to be had.

We lay there till dusk, perhaps an hour, when the fighting ceased. During that hour, while the bullets snipped the leaves from a young locust tree growing at the edge of the hollow and powdered us with the fragments, we had time to speculate on many things—among others, on the impatience with which men clamor, in dull times, to be led into a fight. We heard all through the war that the army "was eager to be led against the enemy." It must have been so, for truthful correspondents said so, and editors confirmed it. But when you came to hunt for this particular itch, it was always the next regiment that had it. The truth is, when bullets are whacking against tree trunks and solid shot are cracking skulls like eggshells, the consuming passion in the breast of the average man is to get out of the way. Between the physical fear of going forward and the moral fear of turning back, there is a predicament of exceptional awkwardness from which a hidden hole in the ground would be a wonderfully welcome outlet.

Night fell, preventing further struggle. Of 600 men of the regiment who crossed the creek at 3 o'clock that afternoon, 45 were killed and 176 wounded. The Confederates held possession of that part of the field over which we had moved, and just after dusk they sent out detachments to collect arms and bring in prisoners. When they came to our hollow, all the unwounded and slightly wounded there were marched to the rear—prisoners of the 15th Georgia. We slept on the ground that night without protection of any kind; for, with a recklessness quite common throughout the war, we had thrown away every incumbrance on going into the fight.

From "With Burnside at Antietam," David I. Thompson, in *Battles and Leaders of the Civil War,* The Century Co., 1884-88.

December 5th–February 5, 1864—Nothing of importance has occurred for some time except the execution of a private from the 4th Maine "for cowardice in the presence of the enemy." Doubtless there are cases of desertion so glaringly aggravating that they should be dealt with summarily, but no man should be shot like a dog for cowardice, this not being a matter within the control of the individual. Some will, I'm sure, urge that a coward of this type shouldn't enlist. This would be good logic if it could be shown that all men know themselves. But they do not. Men are moved by great popular currents, and enthusiasm of this kind is often mistaken for courage. We cannot judge men by the mere fact of enlistment. They are honest and patriotic and no doubt meant to do all they enlisted to do, but it is one thing to talk about "staring Death out of countenance," and quite another to do it. Alas for human calculations, they so often miscarry.

From *The Rebel Yell and the Yankee Hurrah: The Civil War Journal of a Maine Volunteer,* Down East Books, 1985

September 27, 1863—Camp near Orange Court House, Va.,—We had nine more military executions in our division yesterday—one man from Thomas' Brigade, one from Scales' and seven from Lane's.

Colonel Hunt was a member of the court-martial which sentenced them, and he tells me that one of the men from Lane's Brigade was a brother of your preacher, and that the two looked very much alike. He said he was a very intelligent man, and gave as his reason for deserting that the editorials in the Raleigh *Standard* had convinced him that Jeff Davis was a tyrant and that the Confederate cause was wrong. I am surprised that the editor of that miserable little journal is allowed to go at large. It is most unfortunate that this thing of shooting men for desertion was not begun sooner. Many lives would have been saved by it, because a great many men will now have to be shot before the trouble can be stopped. . . .

From *A Confederate Surgeon's Letters to His Wife,* Spencer G. Welch, Neale, 1911.